CHANGE
YOUR WORDS,
CHANGE
YOUR LIFE

CHANGE
YOUR WORDS,
CHANGE
YOUR LIFE

UNDERSTANDING THE POWER
OF EVERY WORD YOU SPEAK

JOYCE MEYER

Faith
Words

New York   Boston   Nashville

FaithWords
Hachette Book Group
237 Park Avenue
New York, NY 10017

www.faithwords.com

Printed in the United States of America

RRD-C

First trade edition: October 2013

10 9 8 7 6 5 4 3 2 1

FaithWords is a division of Hachette Book Group, Inc.
The FaithWords name and logo are trademarks of Hachette Book Group, Inc.

The Hachette Speakers Bureau provides a wide range of authors for speaking events. To find out more, go to www.hachettespeakersbureau.com or call (866) 376-6591.

The publisher is not responsible for websites (or their content) that are not owned by the publisher.

The Library of Congress has cataloged the hardcover edition as follows:
Meyer, Joyce, 1943–
   Change your words, change your life / Joyce Meyer. — 1st ed.
     p. cm.
   Summary: "Joyce Meyer discusses the power of words and provides a guide to 'smart talk' that can change your life"—Provided by the publisher.
     ISBN 978-0-446-53857-2
   1. Language and languages—Religious aspects—Christianity.   2. Rhetoric—Religious aspects—Christianity.   3. Communication—Religious aspects—Christianity.   I. Title.
     BR115.L25 M49 2012
     248.401'4—dc23

                                                                              2011045273

ISBN 978-1-4555-4910-8 (pbk.)

Words can poison, words can heal.
Words start and fight wars, but words make peace.
Words lead men to the pinnacles of good
And words can plunge men to the depths of evil.
—Marguerite Schumann

ix

CONTENTS

PART II

INTRODUCTION

Most of us don't realize how powerful words are and how huge an impact they have on our lives. Think about it. Even two simple syllables—*Da-da*—are powerful enough to make a grown man cry when uttered for the first time by his baby.

I believe that words contain tremendous power: it can be either positive, constructive power or negative, destructive power.

In Genesis, we read that God used words to create the world we live in. The Bible says in Proverbs 18:21 that *the power of life and death are in the tongue.* That is an amazing statement and one that we should seriously consider. Each time we speak words, we are speaking either life or death to those who hear us and to ourselves. So we need to be cautious about the words we utter.

Our mouth gives expression to what we want, think, and feel; therefore, it reveals a great deal about the one who is speaking. We can learn a lot about ourselves just by listening to the things that we say. Matthew 12:34–35 says that "out of the heart the mouth speaks. The good man from his inner good treasure flings forth good things, and the evil man out of his inner evil storehouse flings forth evil things." Our words are the result of our inner thoughts and attitudes. One might say that our words are a movie screen that reveals what we have been thinking and the attitudes that we have.

I believe that our words can increase or decrease our level of joy. They can affect the answers to our prayers, and have a positive or negative effect on our future. We should pay a lot of attention to what the Word of God has to teach us about the power of our words. When a person isn't satisfied with the condition of her life, it would be wise to take an inventory of the words she has spoken.

God has a good plan for each one of us, but it won't automatically happen without our cooperation. We are partners with God in this life, and He wants us to be in agreement with what He has spoken about us in His Word. As you read this book, I believe you will gain new insight into the fact that as you change your words, you can change your life.

PART I

CHAPTER

1

The Impact of Words

Therese was a fabulous worker, friend, and colleague. Everyone in her office loved her—from her bosses to the cleaning lady. She always had a kind word for everyone. One of her best assets was her amazing ability to help people feel good about themselves. She could make someone whose feelings had been hurt feel like they were the best thing since sliced bread. She could make an insecure colleague feel like a genius. Her sense of humor always lifted others' moods and made them laugh even if they were annoyed or unhappy. Not only that, but she was smart—very smart. In her five years on the job, she had received three promotions, and her employer had recently told her that she was on a fast track toward a management position. If things continued the way they were going, she could even expect a vice-presidency within just a few years.

One evening while working late on a project, she discovered that her boss had made a bad judgment call in a speech that he had written and asked her to edit. He had included a foolish joke that some could find offensive. Therese picked up the phone to leave him a voice mail and tell him her thoughts. "What were you thinking, boss?" she said. "Don't you know the CEO will hate that joke? And he has no sense of humor."

Unfortunately, instead of sending the voice mail to her boss, Therese inadvertently pressed a button that sent the voice mail to everyone in the company. The next morning, chaos ensued. While Therese wasn't fired, she didn't get that next promotion—or the one after. The push of a button had sealed her future at the company.

That's an extreme incident, but there are many others today that have far greater consequences. Children no longer tease one another; they bully each other, and bullying isn't an exception among students—it's the norm. It doesn't just happen at school or play; it happens on the Internet, too. In fact, a new word has entered our vocabulary: *cyberbullying*. Facebook is now sometimes used as a weapon.

Never in the history of the world have words been so cheap, quick, irrevocable, and viral. Through cell phones and the Internet, we now have texting, e-mail, instant messaging, blogs, Facebook, Twitter, and YouTube. In addition, we have radio, television, and printed media. Words are flying around in the atmosphere like never before. As of June 2010, 77.2 percent of all Americans use the Internet (267 million people). One quarter of the world's population is online. Forty-one percent of all Americans actively maintain a profile page on Facebook, which generates one *billion* pieces of content every single *day*. U.S. awareness of Twitter has exploded from 5 percent in 2008 to 87 percent in 2010, and by now the figures are even greater. In 2010, more than 17 million Americans used

Twitter and the average number of "tweets" per day in the United States alone was 15.5 million.

Obviously, there are good uses of all these forms of communication; however, there are many disturbing consequences, including online bullying that has led to teenage suicide, identity theft, child safety risk, pornography addiction, and ruined careers. Job applicants lose out because of Facebook accounts of bad behavior; workers send ill-advised e-mails before thinking.

People have destroyed relationships by typing their most secret thoughts in e-mail and then pressing Send before realizing how revealing the message was. Owing to the information available today, personal privacy has all but vanished. Sadly, anyone can say anything about an individual—whether it is true or not—and it is out there floating around in cyberspace just waiting for someone to access the information. People's reputations have been destroyed by what others have said and yet their words held no truth at all. You might say that we have a "word explosion" going on, and we have yet to see what damage will be caused by it unless people learn the power of words and make a commitment to use them in a godly way.

We Eat Our Words...

I am sure you have heard someone say, "You are going to eat those words." It may sound like a mere statement to us, but in reality we do eat our words. What we say not only affects others, but also affects us.

Words are wonderful when used in a proper way. They can encourage, edify, and give confidence to the hearer. A right word spoken at the right time can actually be life changing.

> A man has joy in making an apt answer, and a word spoken at the right moment—how good it is!   *Proverbs 15:23*

We can literally increase our own joy by speaking right words. We can also upset ourselves by talking unnecessarily about our problems or things that have hurt us in relationships. Not too long ago I had a disappointing situation take place with someone I considered to be a close friend and I noticed that each time I talked about it, I would have a difficult time getting it off my mind for the remainder of the day. I finally realized that if I wanted to get over it, I was going to have to stop mentally and verbally going over it again and again. People kept asking me about the situation out of genuine concern, but I ultimately realized that I had to answer, "It is better for me if I just don't talk about it."

The words that come out of our mouths go into our own ears as well as other people's, and then they drop down into our soul, where they give us either joy or sadness, peace or upset, depending on the types of words we have spoken. Our words can even oppress our spirit. God desires that our spirit be light and free so it can function properly, not heavy and oppressed.

When we understand the power of words and realize that we can choose what we think and speak, our lives can be transformed. Our words are not forced on us; they formulate in our thoughts and then we speak them. We can learn to choose our thoughts, to resist wrong ones and think on good, healthy, and right ones. Where the mind goes, the man follows. We could also say, where the mind goes, the mouth follows!

You don't even have to be talking to someone to increase your joy with your words. The mere confession of good things is enough to cheer you up. I have written a great deal about the power of confessing God's Word out loud, and I will continue to do so because it has been one of the most helpful things I have done in my life.

When you get up in the morning, if there is something you need to attend to that day that you're not looking forward to, you can say, "I dread this day," or you can say, "God will give me strength today to do whatever I need to do and to do it with joy." Which of these two statements do you think would better prepare you for the day?

"A wholesome tongue is a tree of life," says Proverbs 15:4 (NKJV). According to scripture, God has given His children a new nature, and we are taught to daily renew our mind and attitude. Having a positive outlook on life and speaking positive words are two of the most wholesome things we can do.

From the fruit of his words a man shall be satisfied with good.   *Proverbs 12:14a*

A good man eats good from the fruit of his mouth.   *Proverbs 13:2a*

A man's [moral] self shall be filled with the fruit of his mouth; and with the consequence of his words he must be satisfied [whether good or evil].   *Proverbs 18:20*

So Choose Your Food Carefully

Anyone who wants to be healthy is careful to choose quality food that will provide good nutrition. If we want to be healthy in our soul and spirit, we should also choose to take in words that will build us up and increase our peace and joy. As we have seen, we eat our words, and we can rightfully say that they are food for our souls.

The world is filled with bad news. Turn on any news station or buy any newspaper or news magazine and you will find it filled with reports of murder, theft, wars, famine, and all kinds of horribly tragic events. And although these things are prevalent in the world today, I do wish with all my heart that we had some "Good News" stations and newspapers. I believe there are many good things happening in the world and probably there is more good than bad, but the evil is magnified in a way that often seems overwhelming. Although we may want to know what is going on in the world, we should not have a steady diet of "bad news," but we should choose to read, watch, and talk about good things.

Fortunately, we don't have to wait for someone else to cheer us up! We can do it with our own words by what we choose to talk about. I recently walked into a room and heard a group of people talking about several businesses that had recently filed for bankruptcy. Then they mentioned two others that they had heard were going to file for bankruptcy. I felt a gloom hanging in the atmosphere so I said, "Well, God is not bankrupt and He is on our side." Immediately the atmosphere changed and everyone agreed with me.

I am not suggesting at all that we deny reality, but we can choose what we want to talk about. If we are not helping ourselves or anyone else by rehearsing all the bad things going on in the world, then why fill our conversation with it? I realize we are going to talk about conditions in the world to a certain degree. We want to be well informed of what is going on. There is no wisdom in being ignorant and taken by surprise, but to talk about it excessively or with no purpose merely creates a gloomy atmosphere that nobody will enjoy.

Thinking About What You Talk About

We talk a lot and quite often pay no attention to what we are saying, let alone think seriously about the impact of our words. I want to encourage you to take some time and think about the types of things you usually talk about. What kind of conversation do you enjoy and participate in? If we are honest with ourselves, we may find that some of our bad moods are directly linked to our conversation. Even some of our problems can be linked to bad choices we make about what we say. As we progress in this book, you will learn that words have so much power that they can actually create circumstances in our lives. For example, if a man continually says, "I can't control my appetite," he'll believe he can't, and therefore he won't control it. If a woman says, "I will never have any money or own nice things," she may end up living far below the level that God desires for her simply because she won't even try to do better. We believe more of what we say than we believe what anyone else says to us. This is very important, so I want to repeat it: You believe what you say more than you believe what others say to you. Think about it. When someone compliments you when you're wearing a dress that you don't particularly like and you're having a bad hair day, do you believe her? Or do you believe that little voice inside that says, "She's just being nice, because you don't look good; you look terrible."

If we say a thing often enough, silently in our hearts or verbally, we will believe it whether or not it's true. And the Bible teaches us that we receive what we believe. All of God's promises are received through believing them. Actually, *believe* means "to receive," and *receive* means "to believe." Believing and receiving are like conjoined twins. The two cannot be separated. What we believe becomes our reality!

It would be a wise exercise to take a little time at the end of each day and think about what we talked about that day. Certainly anytime we are feeling a bit gloomy, we should ask ourselves immediately, "What have I been talking about?" Our words don't cause all of our problems, but they do cause a great deal of them and they should be given a good deal of consideration when we are looking for answers to the problems we encounter in life. We all have challenges in life, but we can make them better or worse by the way we talk about them.

What kind of conversation do you have around the lunch table at work? While riding to work in the car pool? Chatting with friends at a social gathering? Why not decide each day before you even go out of the house that you are only going to talk about things that benefit you and everyone who hears you? Since we have the power to make our day better, we would be foolish indeed if we didn't do it.

Let me clearly say that I don't believe we can change all of our circumstances into pleasant ones by making positive confessions, but I do believe many of them will change according to God's will. I only want to teach you to be in agreement with God and learn to say what He says. For example, God would never say, "This bad circumstance is too much for me; it is just too hard and I am going to give up." You might be thinking right now, "Well, of course God wouldn't say that!" So then why do you? God is in control, not us; however, we can cooperate with His will or hinder it by agreeing or disagreeing with His Word. One thing is for sure: Speaking negatively could hurt you, but speaking positively never will, so why not go with the positive and see what kind of results you get?

Seedtime and Harvest

In the Bible we learn the principle of sowing and reaping. Beginning in Genesis, God teaches us that as long as the earth remains, there will be seedtime and harvest. We can readily understand how a farmer sows seed and waits for his harvest, but we need more understanding about what I will refer to as "spiritual seed." We can see a tomato seed with our eyes and understand the process of planting and expecting a harvest of tomatoes. We cannot see attitudes, thoughts, or words, but they are also seeds that operate in the spiritual (unseen) realm and they also produce a harvest based on what was planted.

If a person continually sows negative thoughts, attitudes, and words, he will produce many negative results in his life.

Likewise, if he sows positive, life-filled thoughts, attitudes, and words, he will see good, positive results. Jesus said that His words were spirit and life (see John 6:63).

As I have already said, our words affect us as well as the hearer. They touch our soul and spirit and can produce a harvest in our physical body. For example, if someone said something very hateful and mean to me, it would affect my emotions and mind, which could in turn cause sadness to appear on my countenance. Likewise, if someone says something uplifting and encouraging to me, it affects my mind and emotions in a positive way, putting a smile on my face, and often I can feel a flow of extra energy coursing through my body. We are energized by positive words and weakened by negative ones. Words can make us angry or they can calm us down; therefore, they must have power.

A speaker was talking about the power of positive thinking and the power of words.

One of the audience members raised his hand and said, "It's not saying 'good fortune, good fortune, good fortune' that will make me feel better. Nor will saying 'bad luck, bad luck, bad luck' make me feel worse. They're only words and by themselves have no power."

The speaker replied, "Shut up, you fool, you don't understand a thing about this." The audience member was stunned. His face became red, and he was tempted to reply, "You @&&#!!&&&#@!" [something I can't say in this book].

The speaker raised his hand. "Please excuse me. I didn't mean to upset you. Please accept my most sincere apologies." The member of the audience calmed down. Some people in the hall murmured; others shuffled their feet.

The speaker resumed. "There's the reply to the question you asked me. A few words made you very angry. The other words calmed you down. Now do you understand *the power of words*?"

I would like you to seriously consider the following scriptures, for they also show us the power of words:

For as the rain and snow come down from the heavens, and return not there again, but water the earth and make it bring forth and sprout, that it may give seed to the sower and bread to the eater.

So shall My word be that goes forth out of My mouth: it shall not return to Me void [without producing any effect, useless], but it shall accomplish that which I please and purpose, and it shall prosper in the thing for which I sent it.   *Isaiah 55:10–11*

In God's Word we are taught a very important principle: The same as natural seed produces a harvest, so does God's Word. When He speaks it, or we speak it as His children, we will see a result based on the type of seed we have sown. Very simply put, if I talk about lack, sickness, things I am angry about, and problems most of the time, then the "word seeds" I am sowing will actually produce a harvest of more of the same. On the other hand, if I choose to talk about provision, health, forgiveness, God's goodness, and faithfulness, I am sowing seeds that will produce a good harvest according to the seed I am sowing with my words.

A farmer doesn't plant a tomato seed and expect to get broccoli, and we should not plant word seeds of bad things hoping to get a good harvest. Once we truly understand this principle and act accordingly, we can change our words and therefore we can change our lives.

I want to close this chapter with a story that I will never forget, told by a friend of mine.

———

One day, when I was a freshman in high school, I saw a kid from my class walking home from school. His name was Kyle. It looked like he was carrying all of his books. I thought to myself, "Why would anyone bring home all his books on a Friday? He must really be a nerd."

I had quite a weekend planned (parties and a football game with my friend on Saturday afternoon), so I shrugged my shoulders and went on. As I was walking, I saw a bunch of kids running toward him. They ran into him, knocking all his books out of his arms and tripping him so he landed in the dirt. His glasses went flying, and I saw them land in the grass about ten feet from him. He looked up and I saw this terrible sadness in his eyes. My heart went out to him. So I jogged over to him as he crawled around looking for his glasses, and I saw a tear in his eye. As I handed him his glasses, I said, "Those guys are jerks. They really should get lives." He looked at me and said, "Hey, thanks!" There was a big smile on his face. It was one of those smiles that showed real gratitude.

I helped him pick up his books, and asked him where he lived. As it turned out, he lived near me, so I asked him why I had never seen him before. He said he had gone to a private school before now. I would have never hung out with a private school kid before.

We talked all the way home, and I carried his books. He turned out to be a pretty cool kid. I asked him if he wanted to play football on Saturday with me and my friends. He said yes. We hung out all weekend, and the more I got to know Kyle, the more I liked him. And my friends thought the same of him.

Over the next four years, Kyle and I became best friends. When we were seniors, we began to think about college. Kyle decided on Georgetown, and I was going to Duke. Kyle was valedictorian of our class. I teased him all the time about being a nerd. He had to prepare a speech for graduation. I was so glad it wasn't me having to get up there and speak.

On graduation day, I saw Kyle. He looked great. I could see that he was nervous about his speech. As he started, he cleared his throat, and began, "Graduation is a time to thank those who helped you make it through those tough years. Your parents, your teachers, your siblings, maybe a coach… but mostly your friends. I am here to tell all of you that being a friend to someone is the best gift you can give them. I am going to tell you a story."

I just looked at my friend with disbelief as he told the story of the first day we met. He had planned to kill himself over the weekend. He talked of how he had cleaned out his locker so his mom wouldn't have to do it later and was carrying his stuff home. He looked hard at me and gave me a little smile. "Thankfully, I was saved. My friend saved me from doing the unspeakable." I heard the gasp go through the crowd as this handsome, popular boy told us all about his weakest moment. I saw his mom and dad looking at me and smiling that same grateful smile. Not until that moment did I realize its depth.

————

Never underestimate the power of your words and deeds. With a few kind words, you can change a person's life. For better or for worse. God puts us all in each other's lives to impact one another in some way.

CHAPTER
2

Taming Your Tongue

Can you or I tame our own tongue? According to the Bible, it is impossible, so why even try? The truth is that we cannot do it without God's help, but with God all things are possible, even the taming of the tongue. I lean and rely on God every day to help me control my mouth and what comes out of it. The psalmist David prayed a lot about his words. He made decisions not to sin with his tongue, but he also relied on God for strength to follow through. He said, "I have purposed that my mouth shall not transgress" (Psalm 17:3b). "Let the words of my mouth and the meditation of my heart be acceptable in Your sight, O Lord, my [firm, impenetrable] Rock and my Redeemer" (Psalm 19:14). "I said, I will take heed and guard my ways, that I may sin not with my tongue; I will muzzle my mouth as with a bridle while the wicked are before me" (Psalm 39:1). "Set a guard, O Lord, before my mouth; keep watch at the door of my lips" (Psalm 141:3). We can see from these scriptures that David was exercising his free will and being determined not to sin with his tongue, but at the same time He leaned on God to bring it to pass.

We can have right desires, and when we do, it pleases God and He goes to work on our behalf helping us follow through with right actions. I suggest that you study the Word of God in this area. Find out everything you can about what God's Word says about the mouth, the tongue, and words. I also suggest that you begin to pray specifically about these areas, asking God daily to help you. When you recognize that you have sinned with your mouth, take it seriously and be quick to repent. Taming the tongue is no small task, but it can be done, although never without God's help on a daily basis.

When I first heard teaching about the problems that can be caused by not taming the tongue, I was convicted of sin, and determined to change. I went home from the church service where I heard the teaching and had a plan to keep my mouth shut and just not talk. I reasoned that if I didn't talk, I couldn't get into trouble with my words. Of course, that plan didn't work because it was extreme and had nothing to do with God's will. People asked me what was wrong with me and why I wasn't talking, and my thought was, "You are not happy when I talk because I say the wrong thing, and now you're not happy that I am not talking. I can't please people no matter what I do!"

God wants us to talk, and that is why He gave us a mouth. Godly communication is a beautiful thing, and words used properly do a lot of good. God's plan was not for me to say nothing, but to learn how to tame my tongue with His help. I had a plan to go home and try to do better, but I had left God entirely out of the equation. Anytime we think we are going to do anything apart from Him, we are a failure waiting to happen. Even when we want to do God's will, we still can't do it without his help.

We need to always pray first and then wait for God's plan. Never make your own plan and expect God to bless it. I should have left the church service and said, "God, I am convicted of sin by the message tonight. I know that I have not bridled my tongue and that I have caused a great deal of trouble by not doing so. Please forgive me, Father, and help me change. Show me what to do and help me do it so my mouth can be a blessing and not a problem. I ask it in Jesus' name, Amen!" Had I done that, I might have saved myself a lot of trying, failing, and being confused.

One of the things we should pray about each day is asking God to help us speak right things. Our words are very important, and they should be used for God's purpose. We should desire to be a mouthpiece for God, speaking His Word faithfully.

If we are not careful and prayerful, we can unwittingly become a voice for Satan, allowing him to speak things through us that bring harm and hurt to many people. We may be good people who would never do such a thing on purpose, but it can happen if we don't understand the impact of words and how much we need God's help in taming our tongue.

A Tiny Spark Can Start a Raging Fire

Margaret loved to play the piano, and there was nothing her husband, Richard, enjoyed more than settling into his easy chair and listening to his wife play. Once or twice a week after dinner, Margaret would sit down at the piano and play. Sonatas, waltzes, and the couple's favorite tunes would fly off her fingers, and sometimes Richard would sing along.

When Richard developed serious heart problems, he was forced to retire, and Margaret became the sole breadwinner for the family. She worked long hours, often coming home at eight o'clock at night to prepare dinner, do the dishes, and go right to bed.

One night at dinner, Richard looked over at the piano and said to Margaret, "I miss hearing you play the piano." Margaret snapped, "And *when* might I have time to do *that*?" Richard said nothing. Margaret instantly regretted her retort, but she didn't apologize; she'd go back to playing the piano for Richard again as soon as she could get her job under control and start coming home earlier.

Margaret never got the chance to do that. She came home from work a few weeks later and found Richard lying on the basement floor. He'd had a heart attack and was dead.

Now that Richard was gone, Margaret couldn't bring herself to play the piano.

What a sad story and vivid example of the wildfire that just a few words can ignite. If Margaret could take back those few sarcastic words she said in a moment of annoyance, I'm sure she would. But it is too late. How she wishes she had tamed her tongue while she had the chance.

Fortunately, most of us will never find ourselves in a situation like Margaret's.

Most of the time, lessons learned aren't as costly as hers was. An ounce of prevention is truly worth a pound of cure.

Let's look at how we can prevent our tongues from sparking a fire.

Nine verses of scripture found in James 3:2–10 are a powerful foundation for learning how to tame the tongue. Let's explore them together.

For we all often stumble and fall and offend in many things. And if anyone does not offend in speech [never says the wrong things], he is a fully developed character and a perfect man, able to control his whole body and to curb his entire nature.   *James 3:2*

If it takes a perfect mouth to make a perfect man, I am sure that none of us will fully accomplish it while we are here on earth. It is our job to press toward the mark of perfection, and yet the Bible teaches us that we will not attain perfection until Jesus, the Perfect One, comes to take us to live with Him for eternity (see I Corinthians 13:9–10). We can grow, we can change, and we can do better and better. But if we obtained perfection in our behavior, we would no longer need Jesus— and that is never going to happen. We can have perfect hearts toward God by fully wanting His will and doing all that we can to work with the Holy Spirit toward that goal. God sees our heart, and I believe He counts us as perfect even while we are making the journey toward perfection. I am very grateful that God sees our hearts and not merely our performance.

If we set bits in the horses' mouths to make them obey us, we can turn their whole bodies about.

Likewise, look at the ships: though they are so great

and are driven by rough winds, they are steered by a
very small rudder wherever the impulse of the helms-
man determines.   *James 2:3–4*

The bit in the horse's mouth is a tiny piece of metal
attached to the bridle that will force the mighty horse to turn
in any direction that the rider determines. It is a little thing
compared to a horse, which could weigh as much as 3,830
pounds. That's right! Although it is unusual, one horse actually weighed that much, and was controlled by a tiny piece of
metal. The bit actually puts pressure on the horse's tongue,
which I think is amusing since God is using it as an example
to teach us to understand the importance of the tongue.

The next example is a mighty ship. Some ships are ocean
liners and can be city blocks in length, yet they are steered
by a rudder that is very small in comparison to the huge
ship. The message to us is that our tongues and the words
that roll over them are powerful enough to give direction to
our entire lives. A great deal of how our lives have turned out
so far is a result of our words in the past or words that were
spoken to us. It is comforting to know that I can change the
direction of my life by changing my words, just as a horse-
man can change the direction of his horse or a ship's captain
can change the direction of his ship.

Even so the tongue is a little member, and it can boast of
great things. See how much wood or how great a forest a
tiny spark can set ablaze!

And the tongue is a fire. [The tongue is a] world of
wickedness set among our members, contaminating and

depraving the whole body and setting on fire the wheel
of birth (the cycle of man's nature), being itself ignited
by hell (Gehenna).   *James 3:5–6*

A few words spoken may not seem like a big thing, but the
Bible compares them to sparks that start huge forest fires. We
have heard reports of millions of acres of forest destroyed
owing to someone throwing a lit cigarette on the ground.
Such a little thing, but it caused terrible destruction. Do our
words really have that much power? If we are going to believe
God's Word, then we must believe that they do.

According to these verses, the tongue is very wicked and
depraved if it is not controlled by God. It is set in the midst of
our members (our body) and actually has the power to con-
taminate the whole body and set things in motion that bring
devastating results. It can be used by Hell itself to bring
about things that only Satan would desire.

Thankfully, there is another side to this story. Through
God's help, that same little tongue can be turned toward God
and used for His great purposes on earth. It can be used to
preach the Gospel of Jesus Christ and do great harm to Satan
and the Kingdom of Darkness. It can be used for many good
things, and even the bad things it has been used for in the
past can be turned around for good. We can always overcome evil with good (see Romans 12:21). Get started right
away speaking good things and you will start seeing change.

For every kind of beast and bird, of reptile and sea animal, can be tamed and has been tamed by human genius
(nature).

But the human tongue can be tamed by no man. It is a restless (undisciplined, irreconcilable) evil, full of deadly poison.

With it we bless the Lord and Father, and with it we curse men who were made in God's likeness!

Out of the same mouth come forth blessing and cursing. These things, my brethren, ought not to be so. *James 3:7–10*

I have seen television programs showing how men have trained animals to do amazing things, and they always intrigue me. It is amazing that we can train a wild and dangerous animal to jump through hoops of fire, and yet we cannot tame a tiny thing like the tongue. However, as I said earlier, all things are possible with God, and when we get serious about taming the tongue, God will get serious about helping us.

Let's be determined to eliminate the mixture that comes out of our mouth. We may go to church and sing songs of praise to God, and then go to lunch and slander the very people we sat in church with. I can remember doing this myself, and I am sure I am not the only one. I didn't know any better when I did it because I had never had this kind of teaching. But now that I do know and you know, we are responsible to work with the Holy Spirit toward positive change.

Teachers Beware

I have learned that being a teacher of God's Word gives me an even greater responsibility in the area of taming my tongue than other people. I cannot have God's Word coming out of my mouth while simultaneously allowing Satan to use it for his dirty work, too.

Not many [of you] should become teachers (selfconstituted censors and reprovers of others), my brethren, for you know that we [teachers] will be judged by a higher standard and with greater severity [than other people; thus we assume the greater accountability and the more condemnation]. *James 3:1*

This verse precedes all the others we have discussed about the mouth in James 3. There are many types of teachers in the world. Bible teachers, Sunday school teachers, grammar and high school teachers, college professors, and parents are teachers. I have a trainer at the gym who teaches me to exercise, and I would not be very impressed or likely to listen to her if she didn't exercise regularly herself. We all expect those that are teaching us to do the same thing they teach us to do.

God taught me this lesson in a very strong way several years ago. I came to a place in my teaching ministry when I really felt that God's power (anointing) was not on what I was saying, and I was very concerned about it. I finally set myself to seriously seek God about the situation, but after three days, I still had no answer. I was talking to Dave about it, and he said that he felt God had showed him what was wrong. Well, I am sure you know that I was not pleased that he thought he knew what was wrong with me, and I immediately became defensive. Dave didn't argue with me at all, but he simply said, "This is what I believe God showed me, and you can take it or leave it."

Dave asked me if I remembered saying some negative things to him about another preacher's style of preaching, and I said, "Well, you agreed with me!" I still wasn't ready to be accountable. Dave said, "Yes, I did agree, but I am not the one who is preaching and I am not having a problem." Ouch! After about a half day of being stubborn, I finally settled down, and one of the first places the Holy Spirit led me to in God's Word was James 3:1–10, which speaks about teachers being more accountable than others in the area of their words. When I finally realized what I had done, I was extremely sorry and felt I had learned a good lesson. I regret to say that a couple of years later I did the same thing again and I immediately felt the loss of God's power on my preaching. That time I didn't have to search for the reason because I remembered my previous lesson. I immediately repented and have tried to be very careful ever since then to never critically judge someone else who is preaching God's Word.

Not only was I doing what I was teaching others not to do as far as speaking words of criticism, but I was speaking against another person called by God to preach the Gospel— and that made it even worse.

Teachers beware! Please receive this as a word of caution. If you are going to teach others, you must meet a higher standard than those who are not teachers. We will be judged by a stricter standard and with greater severity. This does not relieve others of their responsibility, but it does place a double responsibility on those of us who teach because of our position of leadership.

CHAPTER
3

Learning to Say What God Says

When my youngest grandson was nine months old, I started working with him daily trying to get him to say "grandma." I said it over and over, and he laughed. I wanted him to mimic me, and even if he didn't get it perfect, I wanted to hear him say "grandma." I wanted him to say what I was saying! After several days, he finally did say his version of "grandma," and even though it sounded a bit like a *grrrr* with a *ma* at the end of it, we all got very excited. This has helped me realize how thrilled God must be when we finally start saying what He says.

The apostle Paul told the Corinthian Christians that they were carnal and immature and that they didn't know how to talk yet.

However, Brethren, I could not talk to you as to spiritual [men], but as to nonspiritual [men of the flesh, in whom the carnal nature predominates], as to mere infants [in the new life] in Christ [unable to talk yet!].   *1 Corinthians 3:1*

I have always found this scripture fascinating. We know that they could talk, so what did Paul mean? He meant they didn't talk right. Their conversation didn't agree with God's Word.

If we want to walk with God, we must agree with God. If my husband and I are trying to take a walk together and I am pulling in one direction while he pulls in another, we will be frustrated and not make much progress. Likewise, we cannot pull against God's direction and expect to enjoy life.

Do two walk together except they make an appointment and have agreed?   *Amos 3:3*

Many people walk together every morning or every evening at a set time. They have made an appointment and agreed to walk together. Why don't you let the reading of this book be the time you agree to walk with God fully by learning to say what He says? God has a very good plan for each one of us, but we will never enjoy it unless we learn how to say what He says about everything.

Everyone who considers himself to be a believer in God would say that he wants God's promises to come to pass and be a reality in his life. Yet many believers say the opposite about their life of what God says in His Word.

For example, many people say they feel guilty or they feel unloved, yet God says that He loves us everlastingly and unconditionally. Too often we talk about how we feel or what we think instead of talking about what God's Word says, and if that is the case, then we need to change.

Jesus is the High Priest of our confession (see Hebrews

4:14). He works for us to bring God's will to pass, but can only work so far as we agree with God in what He says. Our confession is merely what we say, and Jesus works accordingly. If I told one of my children that I was going to give them a wonderful party for their birthday this year, I would expect them to be saying the same thing that I said. If they said, "No, you're not," that would make me think they didn't trust me. If I continually heard them say, "I doubt that Mom will come through and give me a birthday party," I might just decide not to do it after all. The power of agreement is amazing. When we agree with other people, it increases our power tenfold, so just imagine what happens when we agree with God.

The Written Word of God

The Bible is God's Word written down for us so we can learn and meditate on it. God wants His Word to become part of us, and He wants us to guide our lives according to it. His Word is truth, and it is filled with wisdom. It is full of life and power.

The psalmist David, who ultimately became a king, greatly valued God's Word. Many of the Psalms that he wrote talk about the importance of God's Word, and Psalm 119 is one of the best. David begins this Psalm by saying that we are blessed if we order our conduct and conversation in the law of the Lord. He is literally saying we need to do what God does and say what He says.

Dorothy, an eighty-nine-year-old woman, lives in a nursing

home in upstate Vermont. Diabetes and arthritis have robbed her of both her vision and her ability to walk. When her niece Irene came to visit her from out of state, she expected to find her aunt depressed and distressed.

But instead, her Aunt Dorothy greeted her warmly and settled in for a wonderful visit from her favorite niece. They spent hours chatting and laughing, and finally, Irene could no longer suppress her curiosity. "Aunt Dot, you are blind and crippled. How do you keep such a sunny disposition?" she asked.

"That's easy," said her aunt. "I've spent forty years learning God's Word and singing His praises. In fact, I memorized much of the Bible simply through years of study. Now whenever I start to feel sorry for myself, I speak and sing scripture and hymns of praise. I'm not sure how my roommate likes it, but it always cheers me up!"

None of us look forward to getting old and losing our faculties. But if that day comes, wouldn't you like to be prepared with an arsenal of scriptures and songs of praise at your fingertips? When we obey God and hide His Word in our heart, He provides blessings in ways that we don't even anticipate.

With my lips have I declared and recounted all the ordinances of Your mouth.   *Psalm 119:13*

We cannot say what God says unless we know what He has said, and that is why we must study the Word of God diligently. In order to know God and what to expect from Him, we must know His Word—because they are one. It is not possible for God to say one thing and do another. He cannot lie and is always faithful to perform what He has promised. Satan is a liar and seeks to deceive us through his lies. The only way we can recognize his lies is to know the truth. Only the truth, which is God's Word, will make us free (see John 8:31–32).

I have studied God's Word diligently for thirty-five years, and my life has changed because my mind has been renewed. I have learned how to speak in agreement with God, and I am enjoying the fulfilled promises of God. I know many people who have the same testimony, but I also know many who, although they would like their lives to improve, won't discipline themselves to study and learn the Word or to speak the Word. It is our choice and only we can make it. Is it time for you to make an appointment with God and begin to agree with Him? If so, then don't delay . . . today is the day to begin!

What Does God Say About Your Past?

Many people are stuck in their past. If they have done something bad or something bad has happened to them, they believe that they can never get beyond it. That is exactly what the devil wants people to believe, but according to God's Word, it is not true. We can recover from a bad thing in our past, and God will even work good out of it. God is a Redeemer, and that means He purchases sin and other bad things in our lives with the blood of Christ and turns them into something beautiful.

Just like many of you, I have a past filled with sin and pain from being abused and rejected. I was totally convinced that I would always have an inferior life because of my past. I thought I would just do the best I could, but I certainly didn't expect anything amazingly wonderful. But I learned from God's Word that I could be completely forgiven for all my sin, and that I could let go what was behind because God was doing a new thing (see Hebrews 10:17–18, Isaiah 43:19).

I saw these promises in God's Word, and then I released my faith in them by saying what God said. I no longer said, "There is no hope for me. It is too late. I have ruined my life." I started saying, "I am forgiven, I forgive those who hurt me, and I let go of what is behind because God is doing a new thing in my life."

Faith is a force that is resident in our regenerated spirit, but faith must be released in order to work. We release it by taking God-inspired action, by praying or by saying what God says.

Recently I was teaching at a conference, and I felt led by the Holy Spirit to ask how many people felt they were stuck in their past. I was surprised when about 75 percent of the attendees lifted their hands. I shared what God says about our past and challenged them to make a decision to agree with God. The number of people who are prevented from making forward progress because they're stuck in their past is astounding. The answer is clearly found in God's Word: "Let go of what lies behind, for God is doing a new thing." It may seem impossible, but saying what God says about us will eventually renew our mind and attitude and release us into the future that God desires for us. No matter what you have done in the past or what has been done to you, I challenge you to start saying, "I am forgiven, God has a good plan for my life, and I will never look back." If we were supposed to be looking back at where we came from, we would have eyes in the back of our head, but we don't. Our eyes are at the front of us, so we can always look forward.

We cannot base our beliefs on how we feel or what we think, but we must base them on God's Word. His Word is the highest authority on earth. It is a mighty sword He has given us, but we must wield it. We must speak it and believe it, meditate on it, and act upon it. Don't spend your life bowing down to your own carnal thoughts or feelings. It is time to live deeper than the soul (mind, will, and emotions). It is time to believe we are joint heirs with Jesus Christ and that we can reign as kings in life through righteousness (see Romans 5:17, 8:17).

The God Kind of Righteousness

There are two kinds of righteousness. The first kind is righteousness through right behavior, and that is the one we are most familiar with. We struggle throughout life trying to do what is expected, and what society tells us is right. If we have any faith in God, we also struggle trying to please Him by obeying all of His commands. Most of us never feel that we succeed or measure up to the standard that has been set. We feel like failures, and in general, we feel "wrong" about ourselves and most of what we do. We compare ourselves with other people that we feel are better than us and we try to be like them, but that never works either and once again we feel all wrong. The feeling of being wrong leads to feelings of guilt and condemnation, both of which press us down in life and cause us to live far below our rights and privileges as a child of God.

We spend our lives trying to get something that according to God's Word we can have freely as a gift of God's grace through faith. I say that it is like trying to get into a chair we are already sitting in.

The second kind of righteousness that is available to us is God's Righteousness. It is His gift to us at the time we receive Jesus Christ as our Savior. It comes by grace through faith. And since it is a free gift, it cannot be earned, deserved, or paid for by us. The gift of righteousness that God gives His children has already been paid for by the suffering, death, and resurrection of Jesus.

God takes our sin and gives us His very own righteousness, and by an act of His love and mercy, He views us as being in right standing with Him through our faith.

> For our sake He made Christ [virtually] to be sin Who knew no sin, so that in and through Him we might become [endued with, viewed as being in, and examples of] the righteousness of God [what we ought to be, approved and acceptable and in right relationship with Him, by His goodness].   *2 Corinthians 5:21*

This is the great exchange! God takes our sins, puts them on Jesus, and gives us His righteousness. Someone had to pay for sin, and we could not. So God sent His only Son, Jesus, to do the job. He became our substitute. Are you willing to say what God says? Will you come into agreement with Him?

Instead of saying, "I am no good. I do everything wrong. I can never measure up to what I need to be," start saying, "I am the righteousness of God in Christ. God sees me as right, and I have right relationship with Him through Christ."

The English evangelist George Whitefield, who lived in the eighteenth century, learned that great exchange when he was falsely accused by his enemies. At one point in his ministry, Whitefield received a vicious letter accusing him of wrongdoing.

His reply was brief and courteous: "I thank you heartily for your letter. As for what you and my other enemies are saying against me, I know worse things about myself than you will ever say about me. With love in Christ, George Whitefield." He didn't try to defend himself. He was much more concerned about pleasing the Lord.

I had a severe case of guilt caused by sexual abuse in my early life, and I probably had to say, "I am the righteousness of God in Christ," thousands of times before I actually started feeling the result of it in my life. However, eventually the truth swallowed up the lies of Satan I had believed previously, and I no longer walk around with the constant companion of guilt. The burden has lifted and I am free!

You might ask, "Joyce, how can I be righteous when I still do so many things wrong?" The answer lies in knowing that God sees you as His righteous child, but He still deals with your bad behavior. He does it in a loving but firm way that will lift you out of sinful behavior. He never expects us to do anything unless He gives us the ability to do it first, so He gives us righteousness. He plants it as a seed in our spirit and then takes what He has planted in us and works it out through us, and it eventually becomes right behavior as the result of the righteousness of God we received as a gift from Him.

We cannot earn God's approval and love through our right behavior. But based on the God kind of righteousness, we try to do what is right because He has already approved of us and loves us unconditionally. We are working out of His love, rather than to get His love.

Keep saying what God says. Change your words, and you can change your life!

Exceedingly, Abundantly Above and Beyond

What should we expect in life? Should we expect barely enough and lack? Or should we expect God to keep His Word and supply all of our needs according to His riches in Christ?

The Lord is my Shepherd (to feed, guide and shield me), I shall not lack.   *Psalm 23:1*

Dare we take Him at His Word and say what He says?

God is able to do exceedingly, abundantly, above and beyond all that we could ever dare to hope, ask or think.   *Ephesians 3:20b*

We often experience great fear in our life, thinking that our needs might not be met. Yet God has promised to provide for us if we will simply bring our offerings to Him as an act of faith. We take some of our money or other resources and give them, and when we do, God sees them as seed. If we continue watering that seed by speaking God's Word over it, we will see a beautiful harvest in due season.

On February 13, 2011, I wrote this in my journal, and I recently came across it:

I have had the word *providence* on my mind lately. It refers to God's care of His creation. He sees needs and wants ahead of time and makes provision to supply them. God's power that creates us, keeps us! There is never a moment in our life when God is not taking care of us.

God desires that we trust Him to take care of us moment by moment. He has His eye on us at all times and never for one second leaves us alone. He knows what we need even before we ask.

Consider these verses and start to say what God says:

Let each one [give] as he has made up his own mind and purposed in his heart, not reluctantly or sorrowfully or under compulsion, for God loves (He takes pleasure in, prizes above other things, and is unwilling to abandon or to do without) a cheerful (joyous, "prompt to do it") giver [whose heart is in his giving].

And God is able to make all grace (every favor and earthly blessing) come to you in abundance, so that you may always and under all circumstances and whatever the need be self-sufficient [possessing enough to require no aid or support and furnished in abundance for every good work and charitable donation].   *2 Corinthians 9:7–8*

I don't believe we can just quickly read over these verses and grasp the amazing promise that they offer. Read them over and over until you have squeezed out every drop of revelation they offer. God will abundantly supply all of our needs if we will simply give to Him as an act of faith. Remember, faith must be released!

God does not need our money, but He asks for it as a way of testing and growing our trust in Him. If a person is so poor that she has absolutely no money to give, then she can give her desire to give, or she can give time or prayer for others. We can always find a way to give if we have a giving heart. When we give, do we always get immediate results? When a farmer plants his seed in the ground, does he immediately get a harvest, or does he have to water his seed and wait? We know that he waits, and we will also have to wait. The waiting time is the testing and growing time. Our faith is tested when we have done what God has asked us to do and we don't see the result of our obedience yet. But if we are not weary in well doing, we shall reap (see Galatians 6:9).

I know that God wants each of us to trust Him for provision. He does not want us to worry or be in fear. God's Word is literally filled with His promises of provision.

There are those who [generously] scatter abroad, and yet increase more; there are those who withhold more than is fitting or what is justly due, but it results only in want.

The liberal person shall be enriched, and he who waters shall himself be watered.   *Proverbs 11:24–25*

He who has pity on the poor lends to the Lord, and that which he has given He will repay to him.   *Proverbs 19:17*

But seek (aim at and strive after) first of all His kingdom and His righteousness (His way of doing and being right), and then all these things taken together will be given you besides.   *Matthew 6:33*

God promises to meet *all* of our needs. He may not give us everything we want when we want it, but He will be faithful to provide. God always does His part if we will do our part, and doing our part includes saying what God says. God never does barely enough; He always does more than enough. He put an abundance of fish in the sea when He created it. He caused the people of Israel to abundantly increase in number while they were held in captivity in Egypt. God is abundant in mercy. He is able to do exceedingly, abundantly above and beyond all we ever dare to hope, ask or think. We make Him too small in our eyes and expect much less than He desires to give.

Give as God has asked you to, and then water your seed by saying what He says about your provision. Make your appointment and agree with God, and your life will improve dramatically.

CHAPTER
4

The Characteristics of a Mature Christian

The Bible speaks of three types of people. First, there is the unregenerate person, the natural, nonspiritual individual who has not accepted or welcomed the things of God into his (or her) heart. He has not received Jesus as his Savior and walks according to his own will. His spirit is filled with darkness.

Second, there is the person who has been regenerated by the Holy Spirit through faith in Jesus Christ but remains carnal (fleshly).

Third, there is the mature believer, a person who learns to do the will of God no matter how it feels or how difficult it is. He works with the Holy Spirit continuously to be changed into the image of Jesus Christ. He learns to say what God says, and he lives a life dedicated to God and His purposes.

I wish we were all the mature Christian, but sadly that is not the case. More often than not, once a person has received

Christ as his Savior, he remains in the immature or carnal state. That means he never grows up and matures in godly ways and principles. The church is filled with carnal Christians. They have received Christ, and they do care about the things of God, but they still act, think, and talk as a child. An immature Christian is selfish, self-centered, and finds it difficult to be happy unless he is getting what he wants in life.

> When I was a child, I talked like a child, I thought like a child, I reasoned like a child; now that I have become a man, I am done with childish ways and have put them aside.   *1 Corinthians 13:11*

If we don't make the decision to put aside childish ways, we will remain baby Christians and will never be of much value to the work that God desires to accomplish in the earth. We are to make a decisive dedication of our bodies and present all of ourselves to God for His use (see Romans 12:1). We must make this decision on purpose, because it won't just happen automatically.

The Corinthians were born again, baptized in the Holy Spirit, operating in the gifts of the Spirit; and yet Paul said that they were carnal. They were controlled by ordinary impulses. They were ruled by their emotions. They were envious, jealous, and there was a lot of division and strife among them. All of this kind of behavior is rooted in insecurity. They did not know who they were in Christ and what their inheritance was. They did not know the hope of their calling.

Paul said that they were unable to talk properly. Just by listening to them, he could discern where they were in the process of spiritual growth. If we were judged by our conversation, where would we be on the growth chart? The carnal Christian is immature in his thinking and speaking.

> Brethren, do not be children [immature] in your thinking; continue to be babes in [matters of] evil, but in your minds be mature [men].   *1 Corinthians 14:20*

Talking too much and speaking rashly are also signs of immaturity, and they cause a great deal of trouble. Many people say things without thinking, and they wound others. They may even open a door for Satan to work in their own lives. We must remember that, even though we may be sorry for something we have said, once the words are spoken, they are out in the atmosphere forever. Thankfully, we can repent and ask God to cleanse our lips as Isaiah did, but words are powerful and should not be spoken frivolously.

God's goal for us is that we mature spiritually and are no longer controlled by our own thoughts, emotions, and desires. He wants us to learn His Word and direct our lives accordingly, and be ready at all times to be His representative on the earth.

My Years as an Immature Christian

I wasted many years of my life as an immature Christian. I believed in Jesus and felt assured of salvation through Him. I attended church and participated in various church activities. I was even on the church evangelism team, and went out into the surrounding neighborhoods weekly with a group of people, knocking on doors and telling people about Jesus. I could tell people about Jesus, but I did not act like Him. My behavior was often very "ungodly."

I was selfish and self-centered, and most of what I did in life was done to benefit me. I talked about myself a lot, and when I did talk about others, it often was not kind or loving. My faults were far too many to list here, but I certainly was not living for God. I believed in God and I wanted Him to help me in my life, but I had never made the transition from wanting Him to do things for me, to wanting to do things for Him. My behavior was not guided by His Word.

I regret now that I wasted so many years of my life in this immature stage. Not only was my behavior not pleasing to God, but I was also miserable. I had no peace, no joy, and suffered terribly from insecurity, guilt, and shame. I tried to find worth and value in what I did, and my life was filled with struggle and frustration.

Facing Truth

As I prayed and sought God for answers to my problem, He helped me start facing truth about myself. It was painful, but it was also life changing. As long as we are deceived, nothing changes. So one of the most important things we all need to do is cry out to God for truth. His Word is truth, and if we guide our lives and behavior by God's Word, we will enjoy life and bear good fruit for God.

One of the truths I had to face was that my mouth caused

a lot of trouble in my life and relationships. Learning the power of words has literally been life changing for me, and it is my prayer that I will be able to convey the importance of the power of words to you. How do you talk? It is time to face the truth. Immature believers speak many negative things. Murmuring and complaining are normal for baby Christians. They enjoy gossiping and are very opinionated and nosy. They easily fall prey to judgmental attitudes even though the Word of God gives a strict warning against it

Most of the carnal believers' problems are rooted in pride. They think more highly of themselves than they ought to, and they don't value other people as God wants them to. Carnal believers are often filled with comparison, competition, jealousy, and envy. These things leave them joyless, frustrated, empty, and miserable. Jesus came that we might have and enjoy life, but we cannot do that unless we mature spiritually.

No matter what level we are on, we should want to grow, but if we find we are still in the baby stage of Christianity, we should certainly make a commitment to God to start working with His Holy Spirit toward maturity.

If we are mediocre and common Christians, it is not pleasing to God. We are not to be lukewarm, wanting to be a Christian, but also loving the world and all of its ways.

The word *common* means "just plain ordinary—of common rank or quality or ability." God has not given us His amazing Holy Spirit for common and ordinary living. A common Christian is not distinguished by superiority of any kind. She has begun a walk with God and she does believe, she goes to church, she carries a Bible, she may even do a few good deeds, but she does not stand out for God. She wants to be safe and comfortable. She wants to be accepted and liked by everyone. Her thoughts and words are not excellent as God desires them to be.

> Great minds talk about creative ideas, average minds talk about things, and small minds talk about people.
> *Anonymous*

The word *mediocre* means "halfway to the peak," yet God's Word says that He desires for each of us to go all the way through in realizing the full attainment of God's promises (see Hebrews 6:11). Just imagine how sad it would be if you were a parent who had wonderful things to give to your children and yet you were never able to do so simply because they were not mature enough to handle them. God has much to give us and to do through us, but we need to grow up and go all the way through with God. Don't settle for average or mediocre. We serve a great and amazing God, and He wants us to be transformed into His image.

Settling for Too Little

The immature Christian often settles for far less than Jesus has made available for him. He does not want to suffer or be uncomfortable, so he does not press through hard things. He is likely to just give up and settle halfway between terrible and great. One writer said, "They have not gained the heights to be warmed by the sun, and yet they are not far enough down in the valley to be frozen."

Some people settle because they have no heroes in their life. They have no one to be an example to them of refusing to settle for less than God's best. I believe God is looking for people who will be stars and heroes for Him—people who go all the way through and show others the way. Jesus did it for us, and we need to do it for others.

You Can't Be a Baby All Your Life

The law of gradual growth rules the universe. Everything grows steadily and little by little. If it doesn't grow, then something is wrong with it. A baby who doesn't grow has what doctors call "failure to thrive." A healthy baby gains weight, gets taller, and learns things all the time. He or she learns to sit, stand, walk, and run, and the baby Christian should do the same thing.

As we go through difficulties in life, we grow. Our difficulties are tests, and sadly, more people flunk their tests than pass. A. W. Tozer said in his book *I Talk Back to the Devil*, "It is a solemn and frightening thing…to realize that about 80 or 90% of the people God is testing will flunk the test." God does His sorting out by these tests. He discovers who will stand firm and make progress even when things are not easy. He discovers who will pay the price for greatness. He discovers whom He can work with and do great things through.

If we are addicted to ease and comfort, we will remain babies all of our lives. Many Christians hear hundreds of sermons over the course of years about the importance of forgiveness—yet much of the church is still angry, remaining as babies who hear and hear, but never apply what they have heard.

We pay a great price to remain babies. Elaine and Orrin were thrilled with the birth of their first child. A baby boy, Marcus was an armful of pleasure: lively, happy, and healthy. When Marcus's first birthday approached, his parents had a birthday party for family and friends. Everyone rejoiced over this baby with the huge blue eyes. His adorable gurgles, big smiles, and appreciation of birthday cake sealed the deal on a great celebration.

Six months later, though, his parents began to suspect that Marcus wasn't developing as he should be. In fact, his size, movements, and physical development in general were no different than they had been when he was several months old. The pediatrician examined him and agreed with Elaine and Orrin—Marcus wasn't making normal progress.

After months of monitoring Marcus, doctors diagnosed him with progeria, a rare syndrome with striking features. Babies with this condition do not grow appreciably in size, but their organs age at eight times the normal rate. These children often remain the size of an infant or toddler, despite the fact that they can live into their teens. Their brain capacity is usually not affected; in fact, they are often very bright and extremely verbal. But they are trapped in a tiny body that barrels through the aging process. An average ten-year-old child will have the general health of an eighty-year-old.

Of course, Orrin and Elaine were devastated. Those tiny hands and feet that were so exquisite became a daily reminder that their son would never develop normally.

Little Marcus has loving parents who are doing everything

possible to make his life rich and happy. His great disposition helps all three of them as they navigate each year that Marcus has ahead of him.

While many parents say that they wish their children could remain babies forever, Orrin and Elaine know what a nightmare that would be. The same is true in our spiritual lives. The fact is, remaining a baby beyond the normal time for that creates a stunted life that doesn't allow the deep satisfaction and progress of normal growth.

Don't succumb to spiritual progeria! Thank God that you have the faculties to grow in Christ and become a fully functioning mature Christian.

Christians grow to different levels of maturity, which is why Christ said that some would rule over many cities and others over few; that some would receive thirtyfold, some sixty, and some a hundredfold on the seed of the Word of God that had been sown in their life (see Mark 4:20). God won't give us more than our maturity level proves that we can handle properly.

Some are willing to go farther than others, are more mature than others, and are willing to suffer if needed in order to walk in the will of God. They are not addicted to their comfort and convenience. I vividly recall a young man saying to me, "I believe God is calling me to preach His Word, but I know it will mean a lot of sacrifice and I just don't think I want to pay the price."

Mark 4 provides a wonderful example of the various types of Christians. Please take time to read that chapter; it is bursting with the wisdom of Christ. Let me give you a brief summary. The first person hears God's Word, but

Satan comes and immediately takes away the message that was sown. I think these Christians are unable to focus; they are easily distracted and often offended by something, which causes them to stumble and fall. A baby Christian may hear a good sermon that he really needs, but owing to immaturity, he becomes offended because the pastor didn't pay special attention to him after the service. He goes away and thinks no more about the message because he is only concerned with his own wounded pride.

There are those who hear the Word of God and receive it with joy, but they do not have roots. They are not deeply rooted in the Word of God. They hear it, but never act on it. So although they have lots of head knowledge, none of what they hear has become a revelation in their life. Trouble and persecution come and they are displeased, resentful, and indignant, and they stumble and fall away.

There are others who hear the Word, but the cares and anxieties of the world, the distractions and deceitfulness of riches and glamour, and the craving for things of the world tempt them, and choke the Word. We must be single-minded and passionate about the things of God.

Lastly we see in Mark 4 that the seed sown into well-adapted soil is the seed that bears fruit. In other words, mature Christians are the ones who hear the Word and receive and accept and welcome it and…*bear fruit!* Each of us must ask ourselves if we are bearing fruit. Are you?

Just as a parent measures the height of his child and places marks on the wall to see the growth over the years, we should be able to measure our growth. Have you been a Christian for twenty years and yet you are no taller in the spirit than when you were a two-year-old Christian?

I still make plenty of mistakes with my mouth, but thank God I don't make as many as I once did. I have recently spent about two years studying what the Bible says about the power of words, the tongue, the mouth, and our confession. I did that partly in preparation to write this book, but honestly, most of it was just because I needed to come up higher in this area myself. God has challenged me to go on a fast. Not a fast of food, but of words. That doesn't mean that I don't talk, but I am seriously trying to listen to and obey the Holy Spirit concerning the words that I speak—and to speak nothing that He would not approve of.

The Spiritual Mind and the Spiritual Mouth

One of the things I say frequently is, "Where the mind goes, the man follows." We can also say, "Where the mind goes, the mouth follows." It is impossible to speak maturely if we don't think maturely. Long ago when I heard my first sermon on the power of words and I made the decision that I was going to keep quiet and followed through and barely said anything, by the end of the day I felt depressed. I asked God why I was feeling depressed since I had just spent the day trying to do what I thought He wanted me to do. I will never forget what He placed in my heart: "You are keeping your mouth shut, but nothing has changed inside you. Your thoughts are still bad and that is why you feel depressed." Actually, when I was giving vent to some of my ungodly thoughts, I guess it relieved some of the oppression they caused, but I was keeping them all in, and I felt terrible!

Our thoughts and our words are powerful! You may think as I once did that you simply cannot control what you think, but that is not true. Your mind is your own, and you can keep thoughts that you like and cast out ones that you don't like. God wants to think through us, but so does Satan. Keep the godly thoughts and cast out the evil ones. When you have an evil thought, replace it immediately with a godly thought. The Bible says that we have a mind of the flesh and a mind of the spirit, so we can either think spiritual thoughts or fleshly ones.

Our mind affects our mouth, and our mouth affects our mind. If we think something long enough, we will say it, and if we say something long enough, we will think it. This is why I teach people to think and say things on purpose. Have "think sessions"—times when you think things on purpose that agree with God's Word. Have "confession sessions"— times when you confess the Word of God out loud. Even if you are confessing a promise of God that sounds too wonderful to ever be a reality for you, keep confessing it! The more you do, the easier it will become to believe it.

CHAPTER
5

What Do You Want in the Future?

I believe that God has things set aside for each one of us, gifts that we may never open here on earth. God wants us to receive them, use and enjoy them, but sometimes we fail to understand how to cooperate with God to get things from His realm (the spiritual) into ours (the natural).

> God ... Who gives life to the dead and speaks of the nonexistent things that [He has foretold and promised] as if they [already] existed.   *Romans 4:17*

One of the great privileges we have but frequently fail to make use of is speaking of things that are not manifested yet as if they already existed.

We can reach with our faith into the spiritual realm where God is and talk of the things that exist there as if they were already a reality in our life. For example, God's Word encourages us to say we are strong even if we are weak (see Joel 3:10).

We believe that God has strength available for us, so why keep saying we are weak? Let's begin to speak in faith as God does.

We need to say what God says and do what He does if we want to be what He wants us to be and have what He wants us to have. We should be confessing God's promises as if they already existed in our lives. We are called to walk by faith and not by sight. In other words, we believe what God says in His Word, even more than we believe what we see. What we see are facts, but God's Word is truth, and truth is greater and more powerful than the facts that we see.

> Now faith is the assurance (the confirmation, the title deed) of the things [we] hope for, being the proof of things [we] do not see and the conviction of their reality [faith perceiving as real fact what is not revealed to the senses]. *Hebrews 11:1*

If I showed you the title to my car, you would totally believe that I owned it, even though you could not see the car. *God's Word is the title deed to all the things we need in life!* Just because we don't see them yet, that doesn't mean they are not prepared for us in the spiritual realm and waiting to be delivered to us.

Do you look at things that are and think that they are always going to stay that way? Do you think to yourself and say, *"I will never have any money." "I will never get that promotion at work." "I am afraid I will always be lonely." "I am afraid I will always feel tired and weak."* Or do you call for what you want in your future?

What do you want in the future? Are you cooperating with

what you say you want by speaking as if it is already yours? I know this may seem a bit unusual, but if God can do it, then we can do it, too. We are His children, and He wants us to follow His example.

We should be saying, "I will always have enough money to meet all my needs and plenty to bless others with." "I am the head and not the tail; I will be promoted in life. God gives me favor." "I have an abundance of good, godly relationships." "I am strong in the Lord, He is my strength." Our confession can work for us or against us depending on what we choose to say. Our confession is something that can be done in private during our time in prayer, or even times when we are alone driving in the car or doing other simple projects that don't require our full attention. Saying what God says about your future is smart, but verbalizing all of our circumstances and feelings is unwise.

It seems to me sometimes that my mouth has a mind of its own. It wants to spurt out all of my feelings and every negative thought that runs through my mind. As the Bible says, it truly is like a wild beast that is difficult to tame. Understanding the power of words will help us be more careful about what we say. If you want to keep a problem you have, then just keep talking about it. But if you want to get rid of it, then talk about the answer as if you expect it to manifest at any moment.

My First Lesson About the Power of Words

I grew up in a very negative atmosphere, and as a child, I developed a negative mind, attitude, and mouth. When I began to seriously study God's Word, He convicted me of my negativity and taught me that it was evil in His ears. I made a diligent effort not to say negative things, but after several months had passed by, I still didn't feel that any of my circumstances had changed. I went to God complaining! "God, I have stopped being negative and nothing has changed." Very clearly I heard in my spirit, "You have stopped saying negative things, but you have not started saying anything positive!"

At that time I knew nothing about the principles I am sharing in this book, so I can truly say that the Holy Spirit gave me revelation concerning the power of words. I felt that I was supposed to make a confession list of things that were in God's Word that I would like to see happen in my life and begin to confess that out loud two times a day. I did that diligently, and as time went by, the changes I saw were dramatic.

At the time I made the list, I can safely say that none of the things I confessed was a fact in my life, but they were truths in God's Word. They were things I wanted to see happen, and they were things that existed in the spiritual realm where God abides.

Here is the original list I made in 1976:

- I am a new creature in Christ: old things have passed away; behold, all things are become new. (2 Cor. 5:17 KJV)
- I have died and been raised with Christ and am now seated in heavenly places. (Eph. 2:5–6 KJV)
- I am dead to sin and alive unto righteousness. (Rom. 6:11 KJV)

- I have been set free. I am free to love, to worship, to trust with no fear of rejection or of being hurt. (John 8:36; Rom. 8:1)
- I am a believer—not a doubter! (Mark 5:36 KJV)
- I know God's voice, and I always obey what He tells me. (John 10:3–5, 14–16, 27; 14:15)
- I love to pray, I love to praise and worship God. (1 Thess. 5:17; Ps. 34:1)
- The love of God has been shed abroad in my heart by the Holy Ghost. (Rom. 5:5 KJV)
- I humble myself; and God exalts me. (1 Pet. 5:6 KJV)
- I am creative because the Holy Spirit lives in me. (John 14:26; 1 Cor. 6:19)
- I love all people, and I am loved by all people. (1 John 3:14)
- I operate in all the gifts of the Holy Spirit, which are tongues and interpretation of tongues, the working of miracles, discerning of spirits, the word of faith, the word of knowledge, the word of wisdom, healings, and prophecy. (1 Cor. 12:8–10)
- I have a teachable spirit. (2 Tim. 2:24 KJV)
- I will study the Word of God; I will pray. (2 Tim. 2:15; Luke 18:1)
- I never get tired or grow weary when I study the Word, pray, minister, or pursue God; but I am alert and full of energy. And as I study, I become more alert and more energized. (2 Thess. 3:13; Isa. 40:31)
- I am a doer of the Word. I meditate on the Word all the day long. (James 1:22; Ps. 1:2)
- I am anointed of God for ministry. Hallelujah! (Luke 4:18)

- Work is good, I enjoy work. (Eccl. 5:19)
- I do all my work excellently and with great prudence, making the most of all my time. (Eccl. 9:10; Prov. 22:29; Eph. 5:15–16)
- I am a teacher of the Word. (Matt. 28:19; Rom. 12:7)
- I love to bless people and to spread the Gospel. (Matt. 28:19–20)
- I have compassion and understanding for all people. (Mark 16:18)
- I lay hands on the sick, and they recover. (Mark 16:18)
- I am a responsible person. I enjoy responsibility, and I rise to every responsibility in Christ Jesus. (2 Cor. 11:28 KJV; Phil. 4:13)
- I do not judge my brothers and sisters in Christ Jesus after the flesh. I am a spiritual woman and am judged by no one. (John 8:15 KJV; Rom. 14:10 KJV; 1 Cor. 2:15)
- I do not hate or walk in unforgiveness. (1 John 2:11; Eph. 4:32)
- I cast all my care on the Lord, for He cares for me. (1 Pet. 5:7 KJV)
- I do not have a spirit of fear; but of power, love and of a sound mind. (2 Tim. 1:7 KJV)
- I am not afraid of the faces of man. I am not afraid of the anger of man. (Jer. 1:8 KJV)
- I do not fear. I do not feel guilty or condemned. (1 John 4:18; Rom. 8:1)
- I am not passive about anything, but I deal with all things in my life immediately. (Prov. 27:23; Eph. 5:15,16)
- I take every thought captive unto the obedience of Jesus Christ, casting down every imagination, and every high

and lofty thing that exalts itself against the knowledge of God. (2 Cor. 10:5)

- I walk in the Spirit all of the time. (Gal. 5:16)
- I don't give the devil a foothold in my life. I resist the devil, and he has to flee from me. (Eph. 4:27; James 4:7)
- I catch the devil in all of his deceitful lies. I cast them down and choose rather to believe the Word of God. (John 8:44, 2 Cor. 2:11, 10:5 KJV)
- No weapon that is formed against me shall prosper, but every tongue that rises against me in judgment, I shall show to be in the wrong. (Isa. 54:17)
- As a man thinketh in his heart; so is he. Therefore, all of my thoughts are positive. I do not allow the devil to use my spirit as a garbage dump by meditating on negative things that he offers me. (Prov. 23:7 KJV)
- I do not think more highly of myself than I ought to in the flesh. (Rom. 12:3)
- I am slow to speak, quick to hear, and slow to anger. (James 1:19)
- God opens my mouth, and no man can shut it. God shuts my mouth, and no man can open it. (Rev. 3:7)
- I do not speak negative things. (Eph. 4:29)
- I am purposed that my mouth shall not transgress. I will speak forth the righteousness and praise of God all the day long. (Pss. 17:3; 35:28)
- I am an intercessor. (1 Tim. 2:1)
- The law of kindness is in my tongue. Gentleness is in my touch. Mercy and compassion are in my bearing. (Prov. 31:26)

- I will do what I say I will do, and I get where I am going on time. (Luke 16:10; 2 Peter 3:14 KJV)
- I never harm a sister or brother with the words of my mouth. (Eph. 4:29)
- I am always a positive encourager. I edify and build up; I never tear down or destroy. (Rom. 15:2)
- I cry to God Most High Who performs on my behalf and rewards me. (2 Chron. 16:9a)
- I take good care of my body. I eat right, I look good, I feel good, and I weigh what God wants me to weigh. (1 Cor. 9:27; 1 Tim. 4:8 TLB)
- I cast out devils and demons; nothing deadly can hurt me. (Mark 16:17–18 KJV)
- Pain cannot successfully come against my body because Jesus bore all my pain. (Isa. 53:4–5)
- I don't hurry and rush. I do one thing at a time. (Prov. 19:2; 21:5)
- I use my time wisely. All of my prayer and study time is wisely spent. (Eph. 5:15–16)
- I am an obedient wife and no rebellion operates in me. (Eph. 5:22, 24 TLB; I Sam. 15:23 KJV)
- My husband is wise. He is the king and priest of our home. He makes godly decisions. (Prov. 31:10–12; Rev. 1:6 KJV; Prov. 21:1)
- All my household members are blessed in their deeds. We are blessed when we come in and when we go out. (Deut. 28:6 KJV)
- My children love to pray and study the Word. They openly and boldly praise God. (2 Tim. 2:15)

- My children make right choices according to the Word of God. (Ps. 119:130; Isa. 54:13)
- All my children have lots of Christian friends, and God has set aside a Christian wife or husband for each of them. (1 Cor. 15:33)
- I am a giver. It is more blessed to give than to receive. I love to give! I have plenty of money to give away all the time. (Acts 20:35; 2 Cor. 9:7–8)
- I receive speaking engagements in person, by phone, and/or by mail every day. (Rev. 3:7–8)
- I am very prosperous; I prosper in everything I put my hand to. I have prosperity in all areas of my life— spiritual, financial, mental, and social. (Gen. 39:3; Josh. 1:8; 3 John 2)
- All that I have is paid for. I owe no man anything except to love him in Christ.

I was not talking to a human person when I made these confessions. I was usually home alone and merely spoke them out into the atmosphere as an act of faith. They were all promises in God's Word, so I was simply agreeing with Him.

When I began confessing that all my children would be married to Christian husbands and wives, the oldest three were ages fourteen, twelve, and ten. My youngest was not even born yet, but today the confession that I made thirty-five years ago is a reality. I had never been asked to speak anywhere, but I started confessing that I received opportunities every day. Now I speak around the world daily by television and radio, in addition to traveling frequently to speak at events. These are just a couple of examples, but I am still amazed at the condition of my life prior to making these confessions, compared to the way it is now.

We are told repeatedly in God's Word to meditate on the precepts of God, or to meditate on His Word. To *meditate* means "to roll over and over in your mind," but it also means "to mutter, converse aloud with oneself, or declare something."

You may take my list and tailor it to your life and circumstances. Then meditate on it, confess it, and see how God moves!

Declare the Decree

God's written word is His decree, and we can and should declare it. Centuries ago, a king would write down his will for his kingdom, or what he wanted to see happen, and men would ride throughout the kingdom declaring the decree. God is our King, and He has decreed certain things that He wants for us. We should get busy declaring the decree!

The psalmist David said, "I believed (trusted in, relied on, and clung to my God) and therefore have I spoken" (Psalm 116:10).

The prophet Isaiah, speaking for God, said, "Behold, the former things have come to pass, and new things I now declare; before they spring forth I tell you of them" (Isaiah 42:9).

This scripture alone should be enough to provoke us to start immediately declaring the decree (speaking God's Word).

I suggest that, even as you read God's Word, you form a habit of confessing portions of it out loud. I don't particularly like to read out loud because it has a tendency to make me tired. But quite often as I read, I will speak portions of what I read out loud. I might say, "God is merciful, and slow to anger." "My sins are forgiven and God remembers them no more." "God is my Vindicator, and He will deal with my enemies." When I speak these words out loud, they make an even bigger impact on me.

What was the first thing you said after getting up this morning? You may have set the tone for your entire day. I have noticed that it is really important for me to keep my thinking and speaking right from the time I get up. I am a thinker, and I must be careful that I don't drift off into things like worry, or recalling something someone said that really hurt me. I believe we can prophesy (speak forth) the future of our day by what we say at the beginning of it.

If the direction of a horse can be changed by a bit in his mouth, and the direction of a ship can be changed by its small rudder, then I believe the direction of our lives can be changed by the words we let roll over our tongue.

You Can Bless or Curse Your Future

Most of us don't use our mouth at all for what God gave it to us for. There is great power and authority in words. The kind of power we have depends of the kind of words we speak. We can curse our future by speaking evil of it, or we can bless it by speaking well of it.

Do you have some kind of dream or vision for your future? Are there things that you would love to see happen in the days, months, and years ahead of you? I sincerely hope so, because without goals, we are directionless and very unmotivated. You might say, "Yes, I do have a big dream." My question is, Have your words been in line with what you say you want? When my husband quit his job at the engineering firm he worked at to come into full-time ministry with me, a coworker said, "Dave, do you realize that you started saying that someday you would leave here and go into full-time ministry about seven years ago?" Dave had said something for seven years that he believed God wanted to happen. Do you have that much patience? Are you willing to speak out your dream or vision even though it might seem impossible right now?

The prophet Habakkuk said that God told him to write his vision plainly so that everyone who passed by might be able to read it easily and quickly (see Habakkuk 2:2). He went on to say that God told him the time was not yet, but on its appointed day, the vision would come to pass. God wanted His people to keep the vision in front of them so they did not become passive in their faith. Perhaps you have a vision for your life or loved ones that you need to write down and read aloud often.

Are you aggressively excited about your future? Or do you have a passive attitude of *we'll see*? Don't just merely wait to see what happens in your life, but get some words working on your behalf. Use faith-filled words to reach into the spirit realm and get into agreement with God. Tell God every day that you are expecting something amazingly good to happen to you. When you go out in the morning, say, "Today God gives me favor everywhere I go."

It is easy to talk about how you feel or what the world is like, but it won't help you. I am asking you for your own sake and for God's sake to choose a more excellent way. Speak on purpose and make your words count. It is easy to say, "I feel like nobody cares about me," "I am afraid this is going to be a lousy day," "I'm tired and I dread going to work." Those kinds of words will come naturally, but you can live supernaturally. You can talk like God and say what He would say. Can you honestly imagine God saying, "I'm afraid this is going to be a lousy day"? Of course not! He would say something awesome and positive, and we can do the same thing.

Not only is your day at stake, but your entire life is. What kind of future do you want for yourself and your loved ones? What I say today is building a future for my children and grandchildren. This does not mean that we won't have any problems or disappointments in life, but even in the midst of them, we should keep a good confession if we want to have a good outcome. We have to speak some things longer than others, and we have to speak positive things over some people longer than over others. One thing is for sure: We are better off saying something that will allow God to work good things on our behalf than something that cooperates with the devil's plan for destruction and evil.

Giving New Life to Dead Things

Sometimes we look at things in our lives and feel that there is no hope at all for change. When Lazarus had already been dead four days, his sister Martha did not believe that Jesus was able to do anything. The situation was beyond hope as far as she was concerned. But Jesus raised Lazarus from the dead (see John 11:39–44), and it proved that nothing is impossible with God.

In the Biblical account, Jesus asked the people standing around Lazarus' grave to take a step of faith and roll away the stone that was in front of it. I find that very interesting, because if He could raise Lazarus from the dead, why did He need someone else to roll away the stone? Because their step of faith released the rest of the miracle that was needed. God asks us to do what we can do and then He does what we cannot do.

When we are hopeless, we often fail to take any action at all. We think that nothing we do will make any difference. We may not bother to pray, or we may think that our confession no longer matters so we give up. Are there things in your life that you think are hopeless, or that you have given up on? If so, I am asking you to stir yourself up in faith once again and begin to speak life to the dead areas that need a resurrection.

In Ezekiel, we find a perfect example of how speaking God's Word over seemingly impossible situations works miracles:

The hand of the Lord was upon me, and He brought me out in the Spirit of the Lord and set me down in the midst of the valley; and it was full of bones.

And He caused me to pass round about among them, and behold, there were very many [human bones] in the open valley or plain, and behold, they were very dry.

And He said to me, Son of man, can these bones live? And I answered, O Lord God, You know! (37:1–3)

Let's take a moment before we go any further and really

think about what Ezekiel was looking at and what he must have thought. Everywhere he looked, he saw death, and everything was dried up, showing no signs of life at all. As he walked among the bones, surely he felt it was a hopeless situation.

When God asked if the dried bones could live again, at least Ezekiel didn't say, "No way!" He did leave the door open for God to work by saying that only God knew the answer, and God did tell Ezekiel the answer. He told him to prophesy the word of the Lord to the bones.

> Again He said to me, Prophesy to these bones and say to them, O you dry bones, hear the word of the Lord.
>
> Thus says the Lord God to these bones: Behold, I will cause breath and spirit to enter you, and you shall live;
>
> And I will lay sinews upon you and bring up flesh upon you and cover you with skin, and I will put breath and spirit in you, and you [dry bones] shall live; and you shall know, understand, and realize that I am the Lord [the Sovereign Ruler, Who calls forth loyalty and obedient service].
>
> So I prophesied as I was commanded; and as I prophesied, there was a [thundering] noise and behold, a shaking and trembling and a rattling, and the bones came together, bone to its bone.
>
> And I looked and behold, there were sinews upon [the bones] and flesh came upon them and skin covered them over, but there was no breath or spirit in them. (37:4–8)

Ezekiel had seen marvelous things happen as a result of obeying God. I imagine he felt rather foolish talking to bones. I know I would have. I even felt foolish standing in my home and speaking the Word of God out loud when I initially started doing it. It required faith for Ezekiel to obey God. As he spoke the Word of God to the dead bones, they began to come together, but although some amazing things had happened, the bones still had no life or spirit in them!

What would Ezekiel do now? Would he give up or press on? He waited for God to speak and was told to keep prophesying, and he obeyed.

Prophesy to the breath and spirit, son of man, and say to the breath and spirit, Thus says the Lord God: Come from the four winds, O breath and spirit, and breathe upon these slain that they may live.

So I prophesied as He commanded me, and the breath and spirit came into [the bones], and they lived and stood up upon their feet, an exceedingly great host. (37:9–10)

I am sure that Ezekiel was thrilled that he did not give up when he finally saw the bones come alive and stand up on their feet. Just imagine that scene if you can.

Can a dead marriage be revived? Can anything good come from a past that was filled with failure and misery? Can someone who has been sick most of her life have and enjoy energy and good health? Can someone deep in debt see the day when he can have all his needs met and owe no man anything? The answer to all these questions is yes, yes, yes, and yes. I won't say that merely prophesying the Word over dead circumstances is all that will be required. Obedience to all that God instructs you to do is vitally necessary, but keeping your mouth filled with what you want instead of what you have always had is an important component of your ultimate victory.

Are You Willing to Fight?

Are you willing to fight for the seemingly dead areas in your life or will you just give up? Paul told Timothy that he would have to fight the good fight of faith. Your healing and restoration may take longer than you would like. It may be more difficult than you can imagine and cost more than you ever thought you could endure. But it will definitely be worth it in the end. Imagine how the family and friends of Lazarus felt when he walked out of that grave, or how Ezekiel felt when he saw the results of his faith. Imagine the thrill and feeling of satisfaction you will have if you finish your race.

Staying Strong Through the Storms of Life

When the world says, "Give up," Hope
whispers, "Try it one more time."
—Unknown

It is quite easy to be strong in faith and keep a good confession when everything is calm in life and we have no troubles or challenges. It is quite a different story when trials and tribulations come. These are the tests of life, and these are the times when it is extremely important for us to stand firm and be very careful about what we say.

Trouble tempts us to say and do all kinds of things that we would not do in good times. Jesus was tempted in all respects just as we are and yet He never sinned. His words were filled with faith even as He faced death by crucifixion.

He chose during these times not to talk much, and I suppose He did that so He wouldn't say anything that would give Satan an opportunity.

I will not talk with you much more, for the prince (evil genius, ruler) of the world is coming. And he has no claim on Me. [He has nothing in common with Me; there is nothing in Me that belongs to him, and he has no power over Me.] *John 14:30*

This verse is thrilling to me because it teaches me the absolute importance of not speaking rashly out of our emotions during times of stress and pressure. Jesus had been telling His disciples that He would be leaving the world very soon, and that the time had come that He had been telling them about. It was time for Him to do what His Father had sent Him to do. It was time to take the sins of the world upon Himself and die in our place. The suffering He was about to endure was unimaginable. I wonder what any one of us would have said in that situation. What would have come out of our mouth—fear, worry, panic, complaining, doubt, and unbelief?

Jesus was determined not to give place to Satan by speaking words that would give him opportunity to hinder the plan of God. How do you talk when trouble comes? I believe we lose a lot of battles strictly because we use wrong words. We won't defeat Satan with complaining, self-pity, fear, and worry. We must lift up the shield of faith, wear the helmet of salvation, and wield the sword of the Spirit, which is the Word of God (see Ephesians 6:16–18).

Before I understood the power of words, I wondered what the Bible meant when I read that, "He was oppressed, [yet when] He was afflicted, He was submissive and opened not His mouth; like a lamb that is led to the slaughter, and as a sheep before her shearers is dumb, so He opened not His mouth" (Isaiah 53:7). But now I do understand, and I am fully convinced that we need to follow the same example.

There is nothing that takes any more self-control than not speaking negatively in what we would consider to be a negative situation. The mouth wants to give expression to the soul and spurt out everything it thinks and feels. But in times like this, we need to go deeper than what we think and feel, and think and speak out of our renewed spirit. These are important times to agree with God and say what He says in His Word.

Foolish Talk

Let there be no filthiness (obscenity, indecency), nor foolish and sinful (silly and corrupt) talk, nor coarse jesting, which are not fitting or becoming, but instead voice your thankfulness [to God].   *Ephesians 5:4*

When we are upset, we can say some really foolish things. I had a habit of saying, "I am sick and tired of trouble," or, "Good things never last long in my life." What "pet phrases" do you use when you are frustrated? I know one person who uses the word *death* a lot. She *loves people to death,* things *tickle her to death,* and she says, *My troubles are going to be the death of me.* If I am with her all day, I might hear the word *death* come out of her mouth ten times. She is a wonderful Christian woman who loves God, but she has a bad habit of using language that is unwise and could even do her harm.

Quite often people use the phrase *I hate.* They hate the drive to work, hate to clean their house, go to the grocery story, cut the grass, pay their bills, and on and on. It is just a phrase, but one that carries power. Each time we say that we hate something, it makes it harder for us to do it with joy the next time. Start saying that you enjoy those things that are more difficult for you. Start saying it in obedience to God, and soon you will find them to be more enjoyable. We can talk ourselves into things and out of things. I can talk myself into despising something I need to do, or I can have a good attitude and speak good words about it, and make it a lot more pleasant.

Start paying attention to foolish words and phrases that come out of your own mouth and ask God to help you form new habits. You may have thought previously that it was just something to say, but now that you know that words have power, you will want to make all of yours count for good.

Learning How to Behave in the Storm

As I said, one of the most difficult times to control our thoughts, emotions, attitudes, and words is during the storms of life, but it is also one of the most important times to do it. Jesus met with the disciples on the shore of the lake, got into their boat, and said, "Let's cross over to the other side." Keep in mind that when Jesus says something, we can be assured that it will happen. He didn't tell them how long it would take to get to the other side of the lake, or how difficult the journey might be, and He expected them to trust Him with those details.

When God put it in my heart that I was going to teach His Word around the world, I had no idea how many storms

I would encounter before I arrived at my destination. God knew, and He already had a plan for my deliverance from each one. But He needed to teach me how to trust Him. Even the storms in our life have a purpose. God uses them to stretch our faith and to help us grow in godly character.

For example, patience is a fruit of the Spirit that we desperately need in our lives. We inherit the promises of God through faith and patience, but the definition of patience tells us that it only grows under trial. We may pray for patience, but we get a storm. We don't like it, but God has something good in mind. He is actually answering our prayer and we just don't realize it. The storms of life will be much easier on us if we will learn to say immediately, "Something good is going to come out of this." Recently we arrived at the airport to leave on a trip and discovered that something was mechanically wrong with the plane and we might not be able to leave. It was a trip we were really looking forward to and had planned on for a long time, so naturally the first thing we felt was frustration and disappointment. But thankfully we have learned to take a deep breath and think before we speak. Several of us said, "All things work out for good, so if we don't get to go, then maybe we are not supposed to go." I noticed that my soul immediately started to calm down. We had to wait about two hours, and during that time we worked at maintaining a good attitude and a good confession. The airplane did get fixed, and we did go on our trip, but we might not have if we'd all spoken negatively for the two hours that we waited.

I wonder how many times we get a little storm in life and turn it into a tornado through speaking negatively. I know

I am always tempted to complain when things don't go my way, but I have learned that it is actually a dangerous thing to do and can open the door to all kinds of evil. God wants us to bless Him at all times, not just when things are going our way.

As the disciples began their journey, a storm of hurricane proportions arose. Jesus was asleep in the bottom of the boat and the disciples were terribly frightened. They woke Jesus up, asking if He didn't care that they were perishing. Jesus got up and rebuked the storm and it hushed, then He rebuked the disciples for their fear and unbelief (see Mark 4:35–41). The very next verse says, "They came to the other side of the sea." The thing that has always stood out to me is that they did arrive on the other side just as Jesus had said they would. They could have been peaceful and enjoyed the journey, but instead they let the storm control their emotions, attitudes, thoughts, and words.

Jesus said that in the world we will have tribulation. Storms are a promise! We all get them, and they are one of the most important times in life to keep a good confession.

When storms arrive in your life, remember that Jesus is in your boat. He is with you at every moment, and He will bring you to the other side.

Faith for the Middle

Starting a thing is usually easy because we have lots of emotions to help us. New things are exciting and everyone cheers us on. When we arrive at our destination, we are also excited, but what about the middle? It was in the middle of the disciples' journey that they experienced the storm. They started fine and ended fine, but they needed more faith in the middle. I like to say that faith is for the middle of our journeys in life.

We never know how long our journeys in life will take, but experience has taught me that most of them take longer than we thought they would. Friends of mine have recently started to build a new home. I told them they should plan on everything taking longer and costing more than they had originally thought. I wasn't being negative, but I was speaking from experience. Why does it happen that way? There are always things that happen in the middle of every project that are unexpected and that cause delays. We can avoid disappointment by adding a cushion of time to every project.

People are late for appointments because they don't plan for unexpected things. We would be wise to expect the unexpected. An unexpected phone call may come through that we can't ignore. Or if you're like me, you forget something that you have to go back into the house for. Then you can't find it and have to spend time looking for it. I have had times when I got into my car and could not find my cell phone, so I went back into the house and couldn't find it anywhere. I finally asked someone else in the house to call my phone so I could follow the ringing, and ended up finding it in the bottom of my purse in the car. All that time was wasted, but if I leave no time for the unexpected, I end up rushed and frustrated.

Sadly, many people don't make it through the storms of life. Or they give up or they start doing and saying foolish things and abort the journey altogether. It is easy to begin, but God is looking for people who will finish.

The apostle Paul declared the stand that he would take in order to complete his journey:

> But none of these things move me; neither do I esteem my life dear to myself, if only I may finish my course with joy. *Acts 20:24*

Are you in the middle of a journey right now and a storm is brewing? I encourage you to say what Paul said. Declare that nothing will stop you and that you will not quit. Keep saying, "I will finish my journey and reach my goal."

Here is a list of things we can say when the storm is raging:

- God is my strength, and I can do whatever I need to do in life through Christ.
- God never allows more to come on us than what we can bear, but for every temptation, He always provides the way out.
- All things work out for good to those who love God and are called according to His purpose.
- God is faithful and He loves me. He never leaves me nor forsakes me.
- God is not surprised by this storm, because He knows all things from the beginning to the end.
- I am more than a conqueror through Christ, Who strengthens me.
- I have already defeated the agents of the Antichrist because greater is He that is in me than He that is in the world.

- I am growing spiritually during this storm.
- I will not fear, for God is with me.
- God's timing is perfect, and this storm will end right on time.

Or if you want to be miserable and perhaps never reach your goal, you could say things like:

- I don't understand why this is happening—where is God?
- I can't take any more of this.
- I hate this.
- I am giving up.
- This is just too hard.
- God, don't You love me?
- I am confused; I try to do what is right and look at the mess I am in.
- Nothing ever works out right for me.
- I am sick and tired of trouble.

Which will you choose?

What we say is up to us, but we must remember that our words have power. They have the power of life and death (see Proverbs 18:21). We will be accountable for our words.

> I tell you, on the day of judgment men will have to give account for every idle (inoperative, nonworking) word they speak.   *Matthew 12:36*

When I stand before God on judgment day to give an account of my life, I don't want Him to ask me why I wasted so much of the power He offered me by speaking useless, vain words. I believe we will not only be held accountable to God, but are also held accountable while we are here on earth. We do reap the harvest of the seeds we have sown. We can say whatever we please, but freedom is always followed by responsibility and accountability. God urges us to do things His way, but He won't force us. The choice is up to us.

What to Do When You Make Mistakes

We will make mistakes with our mouths, and when we do, we can ask God to forgive us and keep pressing forward. Isaiah found himself in the presence of God, and one of the first things he realized was that he was a man of unclean lips (see Isaiah 6:1–5). God sent an angel with coals of fire, and with them he cleansed Isaiah's lips and said, "Your iniquity and guilt are taken away" (Isaiah 6:7). Praise God, we can be forgiven and have a new beginning. God never runs out of new beginnings, and His mercy is new every day. Hallelujah! When you first begin to clean up your confession, you may feel overwhelmed by the mistakes you make. You have been making them all along, but now you are becoming aware of them. That is actually good news, because the truth is setting you free. Never feel discouraged when the Holy Spirit convicts you of sin in any area of life, but instead rejoice that you can recognize His conviction and you can repent and start fresh.

Satan wants us to feel worthless and as if we are a big mistake just waiting to happen. Don't believe his lies! He is the Accuser of the Brethren, but when he accuses you, just talk back to the devil and say, "I am God's child. He loves me and I am forgiven. I may not be perfect, but I am making progress and I will never quit trying to improve as long as I live."

CHAPTER
7

Defeating Your Enemies

I suppose we all think that we have enemies. People can easily move into the category of "enemy" if they give us trouble. The unpleasant circumstances in life are also viewed as enemies. But the truth is that we have *one* enemy, and that is Satan and his demons that do his bidding. We can never defeat our enemy until we know who he is.

I was a Christian for many years before I even realized that the devil was real and that he was the root source of my troubles in life. Fighting the wrong enemy and hoping to win the battle would be like having a heart problem and being treated for a broken leg. Your heart would get no better, and your time and money would be wasted. The apostle Paul said that our war is not with flesh and blood:

For we are not wrestling with flesh and blood [contending only with physical opponents], but against the despotisms, against the powers, against [the master spirits who are] the world rulers of this present darkness, against the spirit forces of wickedness in the heavenly (supernatural) sphere.   *Ephesians 6:12*

Although Satan can work through people to wound us, and he can use circumstances of all kinds to tempt and distract us, we must remember that *he* is the true enemy—not the people and circumstances that he uses.

When Satan was trying to use Peter to hinder Jesus from following God's plan for His life, Jesus knew who His true enemy was and He spoke directly to the demon spirit working through Peter.

But Jesus turned away from Peter and said to him, Get behind Me, Satan! You are in My way [an offense and a hindrance and a snare to Me], for you are minding what partakes not of the nature and quality of God, but of men.   *Matthew 16:23*

Sadly, there are times when we all let the devil use us to hurt other people. Unless we are very spiritually mature, he can work through our flesh, and we are usually unaware that he is doing so. We often say or do things that hurt people, or we may create troublesome circumstances through foolish behavior. Satan works through our weaknesses, but Jesus will strengthen us through them if we learn to recognize them and take them to Him daily.

For example, our mouths are usually a weak area for us. We say things that hurt people and cause trouble for ourselves. We will continue doing so until we realize the damage the tongue can do and lean heavily on God daily to help and strengthen us in this area of weakness.

As we mature in God, we allow ourselves to be used more and more by God, and less and less by the devil. We can become a blessing everywhere we go if we will work with the Holy Spirit and learn to listen to Him.

In Luke 4, we see that Jesus was led into the wilderness by the Holy Spirit to be tempted by the devil. He remained there for forty days, during which time He fasted and successfully resisted several lies of Satan. Jesus had a fight with the devil and He won! We can do the same thing. We are winners unless we become whiners! We must be careful what we say during battle. Be sure during battle that you speak wisely, saying things that agree with God's Word, rather than things filled with fear, worry, and complaining.

Wear Your Armor and Use Your Weapons

God always gives us everything we need to enable us to be victorious in this life, and He has given us what we need to defeat Satan. First of all, we have the name of Jesus. There is power in that name, in heaven, on the earth, and under the earth, and at the mention of His name, every knee must bow (see Philippians 2:9–10). Jesus gave us permission to use His name. Praying in His name is the same as if He prayed, for we are presenting to the Father all that Jesus is. His name represents all that He did, and all that He is. I recommend that you read a good book occasionally about the power that is in the name of Jesus. I find that I need a fresh reminder of some of the most important things I have learned. I need to be stirred up in faith once again. When Jesus gave us His name to use here on the earth, He gave us an amazingly powerful gift, and we need to use it for God's glory.

The apostle Paul taught us that the weapons of our warfare are not carnal, and that they are not weapons of flesh and blood; therefore, they must be spiritual weapons. God didn't leave us guns, cannons, and knives with which to fight Satan, but He did leave us powerful weapons.

He left us His name, His blood, and His Word. The Word of God used properly is vital to our victory. We can sing the Word, speak the Word, preach the Word, teach the Word, listen to the Word, and read and study the Word. The Word of God is truth and it is the only thing that will defeat the lies and deceptions of Satan. When Satan told Jesus that if He would worship him just once, he would give him all the kingdoms of the world, Jesus said, "Get behind Me, Satan! It is written, you shall do homage to and worship the Lord your God, and Him only shall you serve" (Luke 4:8). Jesus knew the Word and He spoke the Word. He used the sharp two-edged sword of God's Word against His enemy, Satan.

> For the weapons of our warfare are not physical [weapons of flesh and blood], but they are mighty before God for the overthrow and destruction of strongholds.
> 2 Corinthians 10:4

The strongholds that Paul speaks about are in our minds. They are areas that Satan dominates through lies that we have believed. The only weapon mighty enough to destroy those lies is God's Word. When we know it, believe it, obey it, and speak it, then Satan quickly becomes a defeated foe.

Paul also taught that God has given us six pieces of armor and that we need to put them on and resist Satan. None of the armor mentioned in Ephesians 6 is natural armor made with human hands. It is all spiritual armor supplied by God.

The armor consists of the following:

First, we are given the belt of truth, which is the Word of God. We are told to tighten our belt in battle. In other words, hang on to the Word more than ever in times of testing or warfare.

Second, we are given the breastplate of righteousness to wear. As our hearts are covered with the knowledge that we have been given right standing with God, Satan cannot condemn us and make us feel worthless and insecure. The breastplate protects our heart.

Third, we have been given the shoes of peace to wear. That simply means that we are to walk in peace and remain in peace, no matter what kind of battle is raging. Satan sets us up to get us upset, but if we refuse to be upset, then his plan is frustrated and has no power.

Fourth, God has given us the shield of faith and we are to lift it up. That means we should release our faith in every challenging situation. A good way to do that is to say, "I am a child of God, and my trust is in Him." I also like to say, "I believe that God is working right now in this situation." The Bible says that with the shield of faith we can quench all the fiery darts of the enemy.

Fifth, we are given the helmet of salvation, and to me that means I need to think like someone who has been saved and delivered from sin and its effects. During battle we should remember and say that we are beloved children of God, that we are forgiven and God has a good plan for our lives.

And last, but certainly not least, we are given the sword that the Spirit wields, which is the Word of God. We are also told to cover everything with prayer. Prayer in Jesus' name that is filled with God's Word seals every victory and makes it sure. If we want to win our battles, we must wear this armor and use our weapons. We are soldiers in God's army, and we must not be lazy and passive. We are to be alert, active, and watchful at all times.

Another thing I pray for regularly is discernment. It is one of the gifts of God's Spirit that will help us recognize when evil spirits are in operation and not be deceived by them. Spiritual discernment allows us to know things by the spirit. Thankfully, we don't have to depend on just our minds to know things.

Remember Margaret, the woman who spoke angrily to her husband about playing the piano? There's more to her story. Two years after Richard's death, she had lunch with an acquaintance. This woman mentioned in passing that her sister heard from dead people. In fact, she once had to quit a job because her office was in the basement of a hospital near the hospital morgue, and she had to leave because she couldn't stand the clamor of all those voices! Margaret is a mature Christian and doesn't put stock in speaking with the dead. She changed the subject and thought nothing more of it until her phone rang later that night. It was the acquaintance, who had just spoken with her sister.

"I happened to mention that your husband died a couple of years ago. Then on a whim, I asked her if she'd heard from anyone named Richard. My sister said that she has heard a lot from a Richard lately, but she didn't know who he was."

She went on to tell Margaret that Richard was desperately trying to reach her. Then she told Margaret several things that could not have come from anyone but Richard. In fact, one of the things she said was that Richard wanted to know why Margaret didn't play the piano anymore.

Margaret was extremely shaken up. At first she wondered if God was allowing her to learn things she needed to know in order to move on with her life. She knows the scriptures say to stay away from mediums, wizards, soothsayers, and those with familiar spirits (see Leviticus 20:6, Isaiah 8:19), and she was very troubled. The first thing she did was to pray for discernment. She was in the middle of a spiritual battle. Satan was trying to deceive her!

She opened her Bible and prayed for each piece of armor: the belt of truth, the breastplate of righteousness, the shoes of peace, the shield of faith, the helmet of salvation, and the sword of the spirit. Almost immediately, Margaret realized that she was definitely hearing from someone—not God, but Satan. The minute she realized that, her peace was restored and her awareness of Satan's abilities heightened. Margaret won that battle with God's help. And she has started playing the piano again.

You Can't Defeat Goliath with Your Mouth Shut

In God's Word, we learn about an immense giant that came against the army of Israel, and not one of King Saul's soldiers had the courage to go against him. There was one young courageous boy who believed that with God's help he could defeat the giant. David was a boy who tended sheep and wrote and sang songs of praise and worship to God. God had His eye on David and had, in fact, anointed him to be the future king. The story of David's battle with Goliath can be found in I Samuel 17:32–48, but I will tell it to you in my own words.

David stepped forward and said that no one should fear the giant because he was willing to go and fight with him. Remember that David was not a trained soldier and had no knowledge of the weaponry of that day. King Saul quickly told David that he was not able to fight with Goliath because he was merely an adolescent, and the giant had been a warrior for many years.

David was not discouraged by the king's discouraging words. Are you able to hear discouraging words from others, and yet not be discouraged by them? This is something we will have to learn to do if we are ever going to win our battles.

David immediately began to remember and rehearse other victories he had experienced that were amazing. He said that while he kept his father's sheep, there came a lion and again a bear that took a lamb from the flock, and he killed it and delivered the lamb. He actually said that he caught it by the beard and killed it, indicating that he did it with his bare hands. He went on to say that the giant would be just like the lion and the bear and that he could indeed defeat Goliath. David was not happy that the giant was being allowed to defy the armies of the living God.

Saul finally agreed to let David try, but told him to wear

his armor. David tried to wear it, but could not because he wasn't used to it. David had simpler methods. He trusted God and used a slingshot! His real weapon was his faith in God and knowing how to use his words wisely.

When the giant came near David, he began to taunt and scorn him, but instead of shrinking back in fear, David began to talk back to Goliath. He said:

> You come to me with a sword, a spear, and a javelin, but I come to you in the name of the Lord of hosts, the God of the ranks of Israel, Whom you have defied.
>
> This day the Lord will deliver you into my hand, and I will smite you and cut off your head. And I will give the corpses of the army of the Philistines this day to the birds of the air and the wild beasts of the earth, that all the earth may know that there is a God in Israel.
>
> And all this assembly shall know that the Lord saves not with sword and spear; for the battle is the Lord's, and He will give you into our hands.   *1 Samuel 17:45–47*

Wow! This kind of talk gets me excited. I pray that you and I will talk this way the next time we face an enemy.

Goliath came toward David, and then David ran toward the battle line and he did defeat Goliath just as he declared that he would. David wasn't depending on himself, but he was dependent on God. He wasn't even trying to build his own reputation, but he was fighting for God's reputation. He wanted everyone to know that there was a God in Israel. Are we ready to do battle for God's reputation in the earth today? Will we continue to merely complain when we have a battle to fight, or will we stand up like men and women of God and declare that the victory belongs to God?

Don't try to defeat Goliath with your mouth shut. Speak up, just like David did. Keep your mouth filled with God's Word, wield the sword of the Spirit wisely, and you will be a champion for God as David was.

The Battle Belongs to the Lord

David was not the only one to say that the battle belonged to the Lord. Jahaziel, who prophesied to the Israelites in their time of battle, told them the same thing.

Many armies were coming against Jehoshaphat and his army, and they were afraid. The victory that God gave them and the way He gave it to them are quite amazing. The account of it is found in 2 Chronicles 20:1–22. I will tell you the story briefly, but suggest that you read it as well for yourself.

When Jehoshaphat feared, he was determined to seek God as his vital necessity. He also proclaimed a fast in all Judah and gathered the people together to seek the Lord. The moment we feel fear, we should follow his example and seek God. Don't run to the phone and call a friend for advice; run to the throne of God and ask Him what to do before you do anything else.

We see in this story that Jehoshaphat went to God using right words. The first thing he did was declare how great God is and that he rules over all the kingdoms and that no one could withstand Him. He was praising God and declaring His greatness.

The next thing he did was to remind God of how He had delivered them in the past, and that he knew He was listening to them even now. He reminded God that they had built a sanctuary for His name. He did not mention that they had enemies coming against them and needed help until after he had sent praise ahead of his request. Do you send praise ahead of petition? I think we all forget the importance of doing so at times. We get so concerned about our need that we forget the power of praise. Judah represented praise in the Bible, and God always sent the tribe of Judah into battle first. We must send praise first if we want to win our battles.

After Jehoshaphat told God of their need, he made a very important statement:

Oh our God, will You not exercise judgment upon them? For we have no might to stand against this great company that is coming against us. We do not know what to do, but our eyes are upon You.   *2 Chronicles 20:12*

This confession of total dependence on God was very important. God wants us to lean on Him.

As they waited on God, He spoke through Jahaziel saying, "Be not afraid or dismayed at this great multitude; for the battle is not yours, but God's." He told them to go out the next day and take their positions, but that they would not need to fight in the battle.

The position they took was one of praise and worship. Jehoshaphat bowed down to worship, others stood to praise God with a loud voice, and singers were appointed to sing in their holy priestly garments. This is the song they sang (verse 21):

"Give thanks to the Lord, for His mercy and loving kindness endure forever!"

I imagine they sang it over and over. Get the picture? The king is worshipping, the soldiers are praising, the singers are singing, and the next thing that happened is truly amazing.

> And when they began to sing and to praise, the Lord set ambushments against the men of Ammon, Moab, and Mount Seir who had come against Judah, and they were [self-] slaughtered.   *2 Chronicles 20:22*

That's right! The enemy got so confused that they killed each other, and just as God had said, Judah didn't even have to fight the battle.

This story thrills me and teaches me a lesson that is wonderful. Always send praise and worship into your battles first. Use your spiritual weapons and never forget who the real enemy is.

Always remember these two things: We wrestle not with flesh and blood, but with principalities and powers (see Ephesians 6:12). And the weapons of our warfare are not carnal (natural weapons) (see 2 Corinthians 10:4). Your mouth filled with God's Word is a weapon that Satan cannot defeat.

CHAPTER 8

How Happy Do You Want to Be?

Jerry L. Haynes's mother was dying of leukemia. In two years, she had gone from a strong matriarch to a helpless invalid. Finally, she lay in the hospital room in a semiconscious state. At death's door, she could no longer speak through her dry, swollen lips. Her family slept in the hospital room, awaiting death.

When Jerry woke early the next morning, the sun broke through the window.

His mother rolled onto her side and looked into the glare of the newly risen sun. Then as the sun made sparkling starbursts in her eyes, she licked her parched lips and said, "Gee, it's going to be a beautiful day today." Her circumstances were nothing to rejoice about, but she decided to be joyful anyway!

Can we increase our joy when everything around us is falling apart? God's Word clearly says that we can—whatever our circumstances. And having put the principles of God's Word to work in my own life over many years, I wholeheartedly agree that we can increase our joy. We are not merely victims of circumstance, blown about by the storms of life and having no choice regarding how we will respond.

For let him who wants to enjoy life and see good days [good—whether apparent or not] keep his tongue free from evil and his lips from guile (treachery, deceit). *1 Peter 3:10*

According to this scripture, we can enjoy life no matter what the circumstances may be as long as we know what to do with our tongue (words and conversation) and what not to do with it. The words that we choose to speak in life have a tremendous impact on our level of joy. Happy words can increase your joy. Fill your vocabulary with words such as *fantastic, beautiful, amazing, appreciate, thank you, wonderful, celebrate, enthusiastic, energetic, awesome, great, huge, superb, hope, faith,* and *love.* The well-known worship leader and my friend Darlene Zschech uses the word *beautiful* all the time in her daily speech. It made me happy every time I heard it so I started saying it, too. My friends Chris and Nick Caine of Equip and Empower Ministries frequently say to people while we are out and about, "You are awesome, mate." (They are Australian.) We can spend a day with them and perhaps hear that statement no less than twenty times. I noticed it put smiles on faces, so I have worked that one into my vocabulary also. Notice the words that make you happy when people speak them to you and start speaking them to others. Work cheerful and happy words into conversations instead of talking excessively about problems and using ugly words such as *hate, anger, bitter, give up, my problem, tired, worn out, miserable, discouraged, depressed,* and *wretched.*

The first thing that most of us want to do when we have any trouble at all is talk about it and talk about it and talk about it! I find that I must aggressively resist the temptation to talk about my troubles, and your experience may be the same.

We certainly can and should talk to someone, but the best one to talk to is God and then perhaps someone that He might lead us to after consulting Him first. Some talking about our problems can be very healthy. If we merely stuff everything that hurts and troubles us inside our souls and refuse to deal with our pain and disappointment, it can be devastating. We do need a way of releasing our pain, or as some people say, "There are times in life when we need to vent." I often find answers to my problems while I verbalize the situation, and that is a good thing, but I still need to be very careful about whom I talk to and how I talk to them about the things that trouble me.

Talking just to be talking to anyone who will listen is not only useless but foolish, and it drains our strength and steals our joy.

Whom Should We Talk to?

First and foremost, we should pray about everything. When we pray, we are not only asking God to help us, but we are asking Him to advise us about any action we should take.

> Do not fret or have any anxiety about anything, but in
> every circumstance and in everything, by prayer and
> petition (definite requests), with thanksgiving, continue
> to make your wants known to God.   *Philippians 4:6*

I encourage you to form a habit of going to God in prayer the moment that anything troubles you. One of the best ways to remain in the presence of God throughout the day is to accustom ourselves to having a continual conversation with Him. When we do so, we are praying, for prayer is simply talking to God and listening in our hearts for His response. He may bring a scripture to mind that will give us comfort or direction. It might be an idea, or a strong "knowing" that we should take this or that direction. The important thing is that we honor God by going to Him first. God does not always immediately give us direction after we pray, but my experience has been that He does indeed direct our steps.

A recent situation I experienced was troubling me because it was crucial that I handle it properly. I could not merely do what I felt like doing; I had to be assured that I was making the right decision because it involved other people's lives and I didn't want anyone to be hurt, nor did I want to treat anyone unjustly. After praying for a few days, I felt strongly that I wanted to talk to a pastor that I know and respect and ask his advice about what I was intending to do. It was a situation that had me stirred up emotionally, and I know that emotional decisions are often very dangerous, so I felt the need to speak to someone who wasn't directly involved and could give godly advice without filtering it through his emotions.

The lips of the wise disperse knowledge [sifting it as chaff from the grain].   *Proverbs 15:7*

The wise person can look at all sides, consider all the information, and disperse knowledge properly.

Getting no advice is better than getting bad advice, so the first guideline about talking to others about our problems is that we should make sure it is someone we respect and are willing to truly listen to. Otherwise, we are talking just to be talking and really don't want advice at all. Talk to someone who is known to be "wise," who knows God's Word extensively, who is strong in faith and will keep your secrets. I want to say again that if we talk to someone and have no intention of seriously considering his or her advice, then we are talking just to be talking and that is when our words are being wasted, and perhaps opening a door for the devil to cause even more problems than we already have.

The Word of God clearly teaches us not to seek or follow the advice of the ungodly (see Psalm 1:1). Advice should come from true friends who will not only agree with us, but will disagree if they know that we are wrong. While I was making all the decisions that needed to be made in the situation I was in, I told my husband and two other men of God whom I respect to please let me know if they felt at any time that I was being emotional and not making good decisions, or if they perceived I was being unfair in my judgments.

We should also talk only to people we can trust not to talk to someone else about what we have discussed with them. Only people with mature character can be trusted to keep secrets. The temptation to "talk" is so strong that only those with high levels of discipline in their own lives are safe to talk to, especially if what we need to talk about is confidential.

God's Word teaches us not to associate with anyone who talks too freely, or is a talebearer or reveals the secrets of others (see Proverbs 20:19). Remember, if they tell you someone else's secrets, they will tell someone else yours. Be very wise in whom you talk to. Have you ever been hurt deeply because you confided in someone and then you discovered that person had revealed your secrets to others? I think we have all had that sad experience, and we should learn from our mistakes. Let's learn to choose our words wisely, choose carefully whom we talk to, and make sure we treat others the way we want to be treated. Don't ever tell anyone else's secrets if you want yours to be kept private.

We can protect our joy and happiness by using the cautions I have mentioned so far. I have sacrificed my joy on numerous occasions by simply talking to the wrong people. There is safety in many counselors according to the Word of God, but they must be good counselors; otherwise it is dangerous.

Learning to Hear from God

The more we grow in God's Word and the more experience we have with His ways, the less we will need to go to other people for advice. We learn to hear from God ourselves and be led by the Holy Spirit. Brother Lawrence, a monk who lived in the seventeenth century and developed the holy habit of always being in the presence of God, said that he *had no occasion to consult with anybody about his state. That when he had attempted to do it, he had always come away more perplexed.* He enjoyed a close, intimate relationship with God, he knew God's Word and His ways, and he was eventually able to consult only God when he was troubled.

It is not wrong to get counsel from the right person or people, but we can also develop a close relationship with God that will help us in most situations to spiritually discern what our course of action should be. Brother Lawrence said he had learned that most human advice left him even more perplexed, and I think we can all say we have often felt the same way. Some people love to give their opinion, but their opinion is truly not worth hearing.

God showed David how to kill Goliath. His method of using a slingshot and smooth stones seemed ridiculous to King Saul and soldiers standing by. Saul gave David his armor, but it didn't work for him. He had to have God's direction to win this battle. We would probably win more battles a lot quicker if we learned to hear from God and not be so quick to run to people. But while we are learning to do that, let's continue learning wisdom about whom to talk to and how to talk to them on those occasions when we need to.

How Should We Talk to the People We Talk to?

Once we decide with God's help whom we can talk to, how should we talk to them? How do we talk about a problem and not make it worse?

A man has joy in making an apt answer, and a word spoken at the right moment—how good it is!   *Proverbs 15:23*

Right words at the right time to the right person can be a great blessing, but we must learn the art of talking about a negative situation in a positive way. I find that if I am talking just to be talking, I usually speak out of my emotions and most of what I say is useless. I may be giving other people information, but I am not helping myself, and often find I feel worse after talking than I did before.

Satan will certainly never stop tempting us to use our words to harm ourselves and other people, but if we learn to choose our words wisely, we can benefit and be blessed by right words spoken at the right moment.

Anytime we talk to someone else about our problems, we should be doing so in search of an answer or some wise counsel that can comfort us. I want to say again that when we talk just to be talking and we have no purpose in mind, we usually say things that really don't need to be said. Please notice that I said "we," because I still need a lot of growth in this area myself. Actually, I need this teaching so much that even if nobody were interested in this book, I would write it just for myself.

Do You Have Situations or Problems?

It is good to form a habit of not using the word *problems*. I think just hearing the word decreases our joy and gives us a feeling of being burdened. Jesus had adverse circumstances all the time, but I honestly cannot imagine Him saying, "Peter, James, and John, I have a real problem and I need to talk about it. I don't know what I am going to do, and I am worried. I know I have to die for the sins of man, and My Father did promise to raise Me from the dead, but what if He doesn't come through?" I am sure you are thinking, *That is ridiculous, Jesus would never talk like that.* You are right; He wouldn't. But we do.

He did talk about His situation, but never in a negative way. He told His disciples that He was going away, but that He would return and that they should be happy for Him because it was the will of God. He went on to say that He wouldn't be talking much more with them because the evil one was coming and he had no power over Him. He stated that He had to do what the Father had commanded Him (see John 14:28–31).

Jesus knew when to talk, when not to talk, and how to talk. He obviously knew the power and impact of words. Jesus was facing an extremely challenging situation to say the least, and I believe choosing to say fewer words and make sure the ones He did say were the right ones helped Him get all the way through God's perfect plan for Him.

I wonder how many times we have situations that turn into nightmares for us simply because of the way we talk about them. All of our challenges are God's opportunity to show Himself strong. The next time you decide to talk to someone about a difficult situation you are going through, try doing it in the most positive way you possibly can. You might say something like this: "I have a situation I would like to discuss with you." Then as briefly as possible, give the details and say, "I trust God to provide the way of escape because He has promised to do so, and I was wondering if you have any words of comfort while I am waiting, or words of advice that you feel God might want to speak through you."

In the Gospel of Mark, we are told to speak to our mountains and tell them to move (see 11:22–23), but most of us talk *about* them rather than *to* them. Words of faith will move mountains, but words of worry, fear, and doubt will make the mountains of challenge we face even larger.

Cheer Up

Let's go back to the original question at the beginning of this chapter. How happy do you want to be? I believe the answer lies in how willing we are to discipline ourselves to say what Jesus would say in our same situation.

Jesus told His disciples and us that in the world we would have tribulation, but that we should cheer up because He had overcome the world and deprived it of power to harm us. Keeping our joy and being of good cheer are just not possible amid negative, power-draining conversation. Any person who talks excessively about what she perceives as her problems will most likely be discouraged and even depressed. She will feel overwhelmed, and the more she talks about how she feels, the more defeated she will be.

What I am sharing with you is not difficult to understand. We can increase or decrease our own joy by how and what we choose to talk about. If you don't believe me, test it for one week. Make a commitment to talk about as many good things as you can, and if you have to talk about a challenging situation, then talk about the promises of God and declare that you believe God is working and that you are expecting a breakthrough at any time. If a week is too long for you, then start with a day at a time or even an hour at a time if necessary. I truly believe you will find an increase of joy in your life by choosing your words carefully.

How Do You Talk to Yourself?

You will never be able to change what you talk about if you don't change your thoughts, which are really self-talk. We talk to ourselves more than we talk to anyone. We are thinking most of the time, and those private thoughts are self-talk. How we talk to ourselves determines our level of joy just as surely as our words do. Take a few minutes right now and inventory what you have been thinking about so far today. Our self-talk affects not only our joy level, but also our peace and even our physical energy.

As I said earlier, I have recently been working through a "situation" of my own. I went to the gym to work out yesterday and was surprised at how tired I was. I started wondering why I was so tired and quickly realized that the emotions I had expended on my "situation" had drained my energy. And if you are wondering, I must admit that I talked about it way too much. Actually, it was a fresh reminder for me of just how powerful words are and I pray that God never stops reminding me, because it seems to be a lesson that most of us have to keep relearning.

I happened to see a friend of mine who is going through a "situation" of her own with one of her children, and she mentioned how difficult her workout had been that morning. I know for a fact that she had also been talking too much and saying wrong things. The laws of the spirit work the same for everyone, and God's spiritual law says, "If you want to enjoy life and see good days [good—whether apparent or not] keep your tongue from evil and your lips from guile (treachery, deceit)" (1 Peter 3:10).

We will never change without God's help. Remember that no man can tame the tongue, but we absolutely cannot give up and give in to the temptation that Satan brings in this area. Continue asking for God's help in taming your tongue, and you will keep making progress. Satan wants to steal our joy so he can steal our strength (see Nehemiah 8:10). Why is it so difficult not to sin with our mouths? It is difficult simply because Satan knows the power of right words and he tempts us in this area relentlessly. Don't forget that we eat the words we speak, so let's at least be wise enough not to keep eating poison and thinking it won't harm us.

CHAPTER
9

Words That Grieve the Holy Spirit

To *grieve* someone means "to vex, offend, or sadden" that person. Grief is a strong and very painful emotion. Grieving the Holy Spirit of God is something that we should strive to avoid at all times. First and foremost, we should avoid it because He is God manifested in the Third Person of the Holy Trinity. His ministry to us is beautiful and extremely needful, and we should honor Him and His work in our lives at all times. Second, the Holy Spirit dwells in us as God's children, and if He feels grieved, then we will feel that grief, too. A great deal of the Christian's sadness is directly related to having grieved the Holy Spirit and then wondering why he has lost his joy.

Some of my children's words bless me and make me feel proud of them, while others have at times grieved me, especially when they were in the midst of their self-centered teenage years. Words of appreciation, for example, put a smile on my face and are a blessing to me. Words of complaint and murmuring make me sad. As most parents would, I do all that I can to help my children and add to their joy in every way possible. I do it with no motive except to love them, to give to them, and to make their lives better. I want them to maintain an attitude of appreciation, and it is important to me that they don't complain on those rare occasions when I can't or feel I shouldn't do what they ask. It is not difficult for me to understand that. God, our Father, feels the same way.

We learn from the Bible that an attitude of gratitude is not only important, but also powerful. Murmuring, grumbling, and complaining are dangerous. They are so dangerous that an entire chapter of this book will be dedicated to them later.

Let's take a serious look at what the Bible says grieves the Holy Spirit:

Let no foul or polluting language, nor evil word nor unwholesome or worthless talk [ever] come out of your mouth, but only such [speech] as is good and beneficial to the spiritual progress of others, as is fitting to the need and the occasion, that it may be a blessing and give grace (God's favor) to those who hear it.

And do not grieve the Holy Spirit of God [do not offend or vex or sadden Him].   *Ephesians 4:29–30a*

These scriptures teach us plainly that some words grieve the Holy Spirit and should be avoided by anyone who is speaking. Let's look at the list again: Foul, polluting, evil, unwholesome, and worthless words grieve the Holy Spirit! Here are some others words that I found to define the ones listed in Ephesians 4:29 and ones we might be even more familiar with: *offensive to the senses, stinking, disgusting, harmful or poisonous, profoundly immoral or associated with the devil, not conducive to health or moral well-being, having no real value or use,* and *deserving of contempt.*

The apostle Paul goes on with his message to Christians about what grieves the Holy Spirit:

> Let all bitterness and indignation and wrath (passion, rage, bad temper) and resentment (anger, animosity) and quarreling (brawling, clamor, contention) and slander (evil-speaking) be banished from you, with all malice (spite, ill will, or baseness of any kind).   *Ephesians 4:31*

We see that anger and all of its relatives and the words that come from them also grieve the Holy Spirit and must be banished from us. If someone was banished from the United States because he was living here as an illegal alien, it would mean that he had to leave and could not return. We must exile words that grieve the Holy Spirit and not let them return.

Why Is the Holy Spirit Grieved?

Anything we do that is not God's will for us saddens the Holy Spirit because His purpose in our lives is to bring us into the fullness of what Jesus died to give us. He works with us to bring us into full maturity, or into the full image of Jesus Christ, Who is the express Image of God the Father. We have already seen that our maturity can be accurately measured by the words that come out of our mouth. I am sure you remember that the apostle Paul told the Corinthians that they were baby Christians and he was unable to give them strong teaching, and they were unable to talk yet! They didn't talk properly, and by this and other things, Paul knew they were immature.

Another reason the Holy Spirit is grieved by unattractive, harsh words is that He is gentle like a dove. Doves are very sensitive birds and they will fly away at the slightest noise if they are perched in a tree. I heard the story of a couple who had lots of pigeons roosting in the eaves of their apartment building, and these birds would often sit on their window ledge. Much to their surprise, a dove came one day and rested where the pigeons usually sat. The couple got into an argument, which was not that unusual for them, but they noticed that the dove flew away immediately when their voice tones became bitter and harsh. The pigeons had never flown away, but the dove did. God used this as a lesson to help them understand how their arguing was grieving the Holy Spirit and why they often did not sense His presence in their home.

The Holy Spirit, like the dove, will only dwell in a peaceful, loving atmosphere. We should ask ourselves if our homes are suitable for the Dove, or only for pigeons? When the Holy Spirit came upon Jesus at His baptism, the Bible says He came on Him and remained. Has the Holy Spirit come upon you or your home at some time, but was unable to remain because of angry, harsh, bitter words flying around the atmosphere most of the time? There were many years in my own life when that would have been the case, but thankfully, over the years I have learned the dangers of strife (bickering, arguing, heated disagreement, and an angry undercurrent) and the power of unity.

God wants us to be one as He and Jesus and the Holy Spirit are One. Jesus prayed that we would be one as they were. The Holy Spirit works with all of us relentlessly, hoping to teach us the power of unity and agreement, and the dangers of being quick to anger and slow to forgive.

An unforgiving attitude allows Satan to gain more ground in the lives of believers than any other thing. Our world today is filled with angry people, but we cannot be one of them. Jesus is the Prince of Peace, and He wants us to live in and maintain a peaceful atmosphere. Anger is almost always manifested in bitter, harsh words, and words of hatred and resentment. These are words that grieve the Holy Spirit of God. When we feel sad, we should ask God if we have grieved His Spirit, and if so, we need to repent and ask God to teach us afresh the power of words.

Angry words lead to trouble, so it is wise to learn to control our anger.

Understand [this], my beloved brethren. Let every man be quick to hear [a ready listener], slow to speak, slow to take offense and to get angry. *James 1:19*

If we don't control our anger, we won't be able to control our tongues either. The anger rolls out of us in words that describe how we feel and what we think of the one we are angry at. According to Ephesians 4:31, when anger is allowed to run its course, it turns into bitterness, rage, bad temper, resentment, quarreling, slander, and evil speaking. It sounds ugly when we take a long, hard look at it, and in truth, it *is* ugly. God has created us for blessing, peace, joy, righteousness, and love. He wants us to be a vessel for Him to work through, and that will require dealing with anger and taming the tongue.

Speak when you are angry—and you will make the best speech you'll ever regret. *Laurence J. Peter*

I was once a very angry woman, and of course, my mouth was used by the devil to hurt people and grieve the Holy Spirit. As I learned God's Word and began wanting to please Him with my ways, I knew that my anger issue had to be dealt with. While some of my anger was probably justified, I think most of my anger issues were merely bad habits. I watched my father control people with his own anger, and I also used it as a method of getting what I wanted when other people did not agree with me. I had to face the truth that just about anytime things didn't go my way, and according to my plan, I got angry.

Learning to Adapt and Adjust

If we don't learn to adapt and adjust to people and things, we will break under the strain of life. This requires humility, trusting God, and a strong commitment to being a maker and maintainer of peace.

Live in harmony with one another; do not be haughty (snobbish, high-minded, exclusive), but readily adjust yourself to [people, things] and give yourselves to humble tasks. Never overestimate yourself or be wise in your own conceits.   *Romans 12:16*

This scripture bothered and convicted me until I finally reached a place in my spiritual maturity where I was willing to do what it says. Do you have any scriptures like that? Is this one of them? Are you willing to humble yourself and be willing to adjust yourself to people and things in order to live in harmony? Or can you be peaceful and pleasant only when you get your own way? I know these are very straightforward questions, but I do believe they are ones that the Holy Spirit wants us to answer honestly.

Only the truth will make us free, and as I often say, "It is not the truth about someone else that will make me free, it is the truth about me that will make me free." God wants us to examine our lives in the light of His Word, and since that is not going to change, we must be willing to. If we don't, we will never be truly happy, and as I already said, we will break under the strain of what life deals out to us if we don't learn to adapt.

The oldest man alive just died while I have been writing this book. He was one hundred and fourteen years old, and one of the tips he gave for longevity was this: "Embrace change, even when it slaps you in the face." We don't invite all the changes in life that come our way, and many of them we must simply embrace because not embracing them won't make them go away. Until I fully accepted the fact that my father was sexually abusive to me and that there was nothing I could do about it now, I was fragile and broken in spirit.

When I forgave him and asked God to take this tragedy and make something good out of it, not only did I begin to heal emotionally, mentally, and spiritually, but I saw God do amazing things with what had been intended by Satan to destroy me.

Abuse would not have been my plan for my life, but it was what I got, and when I embraced it, God began to use it for my good and the good of others who had also been hurt. Jesus didn't like the thought of dying on the cross, but when He knew it was what He had to do, He embraced it and trusted His heavenly Father. He wasn't on the cross, struggling to get off. Because He did embrace it, our sins are forgiven and we have an intimate relationship with Him. Don't let your disappointments in life become a place for you to stumble over and never recover from. Embrace them and let them bring you closer to God. Let them make you better, not bitter!

Can You Really Change It?

When you have a circumstance that wasn't part of your plan, or that you didn't invite into your life, ask yourself if you can change it. If you can't, then embrace it, deal with it, and go on. For the many years my father abused me, I often looked at a little plaque that hung in my grandmother's kitchen. It read, "Lord, help me change the things I can, accept the things I cannot change, and the wisdom to know the difference." I drew strength from that little plaque for many years as I was waiting to get old enough to leave home and get away from my father. I think the saying on that plaque is valuable to us in many situations.

Let me tell you a story of how I learned to "go with the flow" in life.

When my children were very young, we always had dinner together every night as a family. I was a stay-at-home mom back then, and I spent hours cooking dinner most nights. I would like to say that those times were lovely family times, but quite often they were ruined. What was the problem? Well, back then I would have told you it was "spilled milk," but now I know it was my anger and inability to adjust and adapt to any circumstance that was unpleasant.

It seemed to me that almost every time we sat down to a meal, somebody would spill a glass of something, and often it was milk. Whenever that happened, I would immediately get upset, and words would start pouring out of my mouth. "I don't believe this! Look at what you did! I spent all afternoon cooking this meal and all I wanted to do was sit in peace and eat it, but you ruined it!" By then, whoever I was yelling at was crying, and that seemed to make me even angrier. I finally realized that it wasn't one of my children ruining the dinner, and it wasn't the spilled milk, but it was me and my attitude that had ruined it!

In those days, we had big meals with lots of dishes and utensils all over the table. When the milk spilled, it would invariably start running under all those dishes and head straight for the crack in the table where we could expand it. In fact, I finally decided that the devil designed tables with cracks in them just to drive me crazy. Now I think it was

God Who designed them (at least mine) for the express purpose of helping me see how foolishly I behaved.

One of the reasons I got into such a panic when the milk was spilled was because I knew that if I didn't get it cleaned up before it reached the crack, it would seep into it and run down the legs of the table and get on the floor. Back then we had carpet on the kitchen floor as many other people did, and I didn't want milk to get into it and sour. Yes, we had carpet on the kitchen floor! I am sure that sounds bizarre now, but it was a carpet that was made for kitchens.

If you have ever had a kitchen table with a crack in it, you know that food crumbs get into the crack over time. Unless you regularly open up the table and clean them out, it can get messy. Add milk to the mix and you have no choice but to take the table apart and head into a major cleaning job.

On the occasions when I couldn't wipe up the milk before it got to the crack, I became extra angry. Now imagine the scene! I'm under the table yelling while trying to clean up the mess with a rag, my children are crying, Dave is probably wishing he had stayed at work, and in the midst of this, God speaks! I suddenly realized, "Joyce, no matter how much you yell, this milk will not run back up the table legs, across the table, and into the glass again, so you might as well learn to 'go with the flow.'"

"Go with the flow" became a major theme in my life. I started learning how to adapt and adjust myself instead of trying to force everything and everyone to adjust to me. It became a primary theme when I started teaching God's Word and has actually helped thousands of others see the importance of not trying to change something that they could not change.

You might be thinking, "Joyce, I wish all I were dealing with right now was spilled milk." I know the example is simple, but the principle is the same no matter what we are dealing with. If we can do something about it, then do it, and if not, embrace it and let God show Himself strong.

When disappointing things happen to me now, I often say, "You lose, Devil; I am staying peaceful." The devil sets us up to get us upset, but we can learn to recognize when he is at work and remain calm in the storm. If we don't let things make us angry, then we won't speak those angry words that grieve the Holy Spirit.

CHAPTER
10

Fasting Your Words

When we speak of fasting, we are usually talking about abstaining from food for a period of time in order to cleanse the body of toxins, or for the spiritual purpose of more dedicated, powerful prayer and becoming closer to God. But there are things we may be led to abstain from other than food.

I have a lot more trouble with what comes out of my mouth than what goes into it. I am very disciplined in my eating habits, not because I am so amazingly disciplined, but for the simple reason that I want my clothes to fit me.

I am also aware that if I gain weight, about two-thirds of the world that can watch my television program will know it! I still want to look as good as I can for as long as I can. I tell God that it is all for His glory and I sincerely pray that it is.

God spoke through the prophet Isaiah and told him that while people were fasting their food, they were in strife, mistreating workmen, not helping the poor and needy, pointing the finger in scorn at other people, and engaging in every form of false, harsh, unjust, and wicked speaking (see Isaiah 58:1–9).

Isaiah 58 has had a profound effect on my life. It caused me to realize that I had many ways that were not pleasing to God, and that there were many things I needed to "fast" (do without) in my life.

I had fasted and learned how to miss a few meals and discovered that I wouldn't die from hunger, but I still had things in my life that were not pleasing to God. I was selfish and self-centered, although I was in ministry and preaching the Gospel. I wasn't doing nearly as much for the poor as God wanted me to, and we still had a lot of strife behind closed doors at home. I had yokes of bondage in my own life that needed to be dealt with, but I was successfully ignoring them by trying to help other people deal with their bondages. Do you know that we are able to hide from God in good works? We can stay so busy going to church, sacrificing time in serving on committees, and doing good deeds that we have no time to listen to what God is trying to say to us personally. God always has, and always will desire obedience rather than sacrifice (see 1 Samuel 15:22).

Regarding fasting food, I do believe the times that God led me to fast my food were very important in helping me begin to see the deeper issues I needed to deal with, and I recommend fasting for periods of time as God leads and instructs. We probably need to be able to control what goes into our mouth before we can hope to control what comes out of it.

People were accustomed to fasting a lot in Jesus' day. It was part of their religious ritual, but Jesus told them what was in their heart and came out of their mouth was much more revealing and important:

> Do you not see and understand that whatever goes into the mouth passes into the abdomen and so passes on into the place where discharges are deposited?
>
> But whatever comes out of the mouth comes from the heart, and this is what makes a man unclean and defiles [him].
>
> For out of the heart come evil thoughts (reasonings and disputings and designs) such as murder, adultery, sexual vice, theft, false witnessing, slander, and irreverent speech.
>
> These are what make a man unclean and defile [him].   *Matthew 15:17–20a*

It is as if Jesus is saying, you eat and you go to the bathroom and it is gone, but the things that come of the mouth are issues stuck in your heart and they are much more important than eating food. What would happen if we spent as much time pondering and planning for what comes out of the mouth (words) as we do for what goes into it (our food)? I personally think a lot about what I am going to eat. On any given day I can tell you by 10 a.m. or sooner what I will eat that day and maybe the next. What I eat is important to me. I plan for it, I pay money for it, I make an event out of it, and I am very disappointed if I get a bad meal.

I think I am finally starting to spend equal time preparing for what comes out of my mouth, but it has taken years to get here.

During those years when I was just being what I now call "religious," I attended prayer meetings, but honestly a lot of my prayers were not being answered. Was it the devil's fault or mine? Isaiah 58 teaches us that there are some specific things we need to examine if our prayers are not being answered.

> Then you shall call, and the Lord will answer: You shall cry, and He will say, Here I am. If you take away from your midst yokes of oppression [wherever you find them], the finger pointed in scorn [toward the oppressed or the godly], and every form of false, harsh, unjust, and wicked speaking.   *Isaiah 58:9*

This scripture doesn't need a lot of deep theological discernment. It says what it means and means what it says. If I want my prayers to be quickly answered, I need to treat people really well, never judge them critically, and learn how to talk properly by removing false, harsh, unjust, and wicked speaking. Ouch! Ouch! Ouch! Does anyone else besides me feel like you just got caught with your hand in the cookie jar, and got it slapped? Do you need to say with me, "God, I am guilty, please forgive me and teach me to obey this scripture"?

The last line of verse 13 says that we must stop speaking with our own idle words. That means we need to learn to fast our words. Don't say words so quickly that wrong ones come out without thinking of the weight of them, but learn to "fast" words.

"Don't Say That"

I have been trying for three years to successfully complete a "word fast." To me, it means that when the scripture has instructed me not to talk in a certain way, I will do my best to refrain from doing so, and when I fail, I will immediately repent, ask God for forgiveness, and seek to do better in the future. It also means that when I am talking or thinking about talking and the Holy Spirit whispers, "Don't say that," I stop immediately and rethink what I should say, if anything.

I would love to be able to tell you that I have had great success, but the truth is that I haven't. I have improved and I am trying to celebrate my successes since I did write a book on that, too (*Eat the Cookie, Buy the Shoes*), but I have so far to go that it makes me sad sometimes. I am reminded that the Bible says that no man can tame the tongue, and believe me, I am leaning heavily on God. I know that I can't do it on my own, but I cannot give up. This is one area where I feel that I must keep pressing onward until I have victory. I am also aware that since I am daring to write a book on the power of words, trying to teach other people to be careful what they say, I may be tempted by the enemy as never before. Why don't you stop right now and pray for yourself and for me, that we will both be able to resist temptation and say only what God would say when we talk.

Over the years I have improved dramatically in what I say and don't say, but for me, this is an area where "doing okay" is not good enough. I feel compelled by God to make this a lifetime quest if I need to. In other words, I have determined in my heart that if it takes until I die, I want all my words to be pleasing to God. Even then I probably will not have arrived at perfection in this area, but at least I will die trying!

Sometimes I am so busy talking that I just plain don't hear the Holy Spirit's whispers. But at other times I do hear and I want to say what I am saying so strongly that I just keep talking. God's chastisement for me in this area is getting stronger, and I am glad of it, because it is obvious to me that I need Him to keep showing me how serious this is.

Are you willing to stop talking and reconsider what you are saying (or about to say) anytime the Holy Spirit whispers, "Don't say that"? I can tell you that doing it is not as easy as saying that you will do it. It seems to me sometimes that my mouth is like a wild animal that gets loose and starts running around and tearing things up, and it is hard to stop it. Or it is like one of those windup talking toys that, once you wind it up, won't stop until it winds down. They are most irritating and I usually cannot wait until they shut up. It makes me wonder if people sometimes feel the same way about me.

I pray you will make the commitment to fast your words, but I want you to know that it may be a lifetime quest. I believe that God will see our heart and perhaps it will make Him smile just knowing that we want to never sin with our mouths.

Study to Stay Strong

I have a collection of books on the power of words, and I also have most of the scriptures in the Bible on the subject highlighted. Many of them I have committed to memory and others I have written in journals. I could never hope to be successful in controlling my tongue if I didn't keep God's Word on the subject in the forefront of what I study. We are instructed in God's Word to study to show ourselves approved, a workman that need not be ashamed. If we don't study, we may even be guilty of telling others what to do and then not doing it ourselves. How often have we said to one of our children or a friend, "You shouldn't say that," or "You shouldn't talk like that," and if the truth be told, we say even worse things ourselves? We can read a scripture once and know what we should do, but we must study diligently in order for the information to become a revelation that will change our behavior.

Millions of people around the world go to church regularly and hear sermons, but how many diligently study God's Word themselves? I was one of those people who attended church for about thirteen years before I started studying diligently. I might add that during all the years I only attended church, my behavior didn't change much for the better. But after I began to study, I experienced many good changes. The apostle Paul told the Corinthians that if they continued to study the Word of God, they would be changed into the image of Jesus Christ (see 2 Corinthians 3:18). Please take time to ponder these next two verses of scripture:

Study and be eager and do your utmost to present yourself to God approved (tested by trial), a workman who has no cause to be ashamed, correctly analyzing and accurately dividing [rightly handling and skillfully teaching] the Word of Truth.

But avoid all empty (vain, useless, idle) talk, for it will lead people into more and more ungodliness.   *2 Timothy 2:15–16*

It is interesting that studying the Word of Truth and avoiding idle, useless talk are linked together in these two verses of scripture. The more we study, the more likely we are to do what God commands us to do.

My Mouth and My Ministry

The ministry that God has called me to is teaching and preaching His Word, so I use my mouth all the time. I often say, "I am a mouth in the body of Christ." If you are a helper, you could say you're a hand in Christ's body, et cetera. I don't think I can expect to speak words of power in the pulpit if I am going to speak harsh, unjust, idle, and useless words the rest of the time. I can't complain about my ministry and all the work I have to do and expect my ministry to be successful and powerful. I can't gossip, tell other people's secrets, and find fault with everyone and then expect my messages on love to have a positive impact on people.

I have seen some really mean preachers who criticize everyone who isn't exactly like they are, and I also have been on the receiving end of some of the most critical, mean-spirited Christians one could possibly imagine, and I don't want to be like them. On the other hand, I have been with some of the most beautiful-spirited people in the world—

people who genuinely love others and never have a bad word to say about anybody. I do want to be like them!

I encourage you to spend time with people whom you truly want to be like. Choose people who will make you want to improve, not ones that make you small-minded and big-mouthed. Spend time with people who use their words wisely, and it will encourage you to do the same thing.

The prophet Isaiah's mouth had to be cleansed before he could be released into the call of God on his life. He was in the presence of God and realized he had unclean lips and dwelt in the midst of a people of unclean lips. He quickly asked God to cleanse his lips, and only after that was done did God release him to go and prophesy His message to others (see Isaiah 6:1–9). Anyone who wants to be used by God in any kind of ministry will need to learn how to discipline the words she speaks. She will need to learn how to "fast her words."

Jesus said, "My words are spirit and they are life." His words were all-powerful. When Jesus spoke, people were astonished, for He spoke as one with authority. He commanded demons and they had to obey; He spoke healing and it manifested. Jesus didn't speak a mixture of good and evil. He was careful about His words. The Bible teaches us that the Antichrist will be slain with the breath of Jesus' mouth (see 2 Thessalonians 2:8).

A list of qualifications for spiritual leaders is found in 1 Timothy 1:1–13, and we find there that a leader must not be a slanderer or a double-talker, but must be sincere in everything he or she says. The list also mentions that women must not be gossipers, but temperate and self-controlled. To be in spiritual leadership, we need more than a gift; we must also have a godly character that has been proven and tried. Our ministry (and we all have a ministry if we are believers) and effectiveness do have a lot to do with our mouths so let's begin to take what we say more seriously than ever before.

Don't Go to Extremes

In my quest not to talk too much and never say wrong things, I have gotten out of balance at times. If Satan cannot get us to ignore a commandment of God, then he frequently works to get us to be extreme. For example, we should go to church and pray and study God's Word, but I have known women who spent too much time doing those things and ignored their families. They became so spiritual they were no earthly good, and their excess made their unsaved husbands want nothing to do with church or God.

I am a talker, and some of you are, too. Our personalities are geared toward verbalizing. My husband, on the other hand, is not a big talker. He talks plenty, but rarely talks too much. In my desire to "fast my words," I became excessively quiet and it had an adverse effect on me emotionally. God doesn't want us not to talk, but He does want us to say right things. He wants our words to be beneficial to Him, ourselves, and other people. Fasting our words doesn't mean that we don't talk, but it means that we choose very carefully what we will and won't say. Fasting means that we are willing to avoid or give something up that we normally would do. As an example, I am trying to avoid interrupting others when they are talking. People who talk a lot are usually more interested in what they are saying than they are in listening to what others are saying, and I want to be respectful to all people. So I am fasting interrupting!

Are there areas where you might be able to fast your words and learn to use more self-control? Some fasting lasts for a short time only; others last longer. I have fasted in a variety of ways for 40 days, 28 days, 10 days, 7 days, 3 days, 1 day, and even one meal in years past. But I think that fasting my words will be a lifetime fast. If you are bold and courageous, why not join me and we will fast together!

CHAPTER
11

Speak No Evil

Don't speak unless you can improve the silence.
—Spanish proverb

Is it possible to never say anything if we don't say something positive? Admittedly, there are things we must discuss that don't come under the category of "positive," but we can learn to talk in a positive way about things that are negative. We can learn to find the good in everything and in everybody. If we make a commitment to look for the good, it is always there somewhere.

> Love bears up under anything and everything that comes, is ever ready to believe the best of every person, its hopes are fadeless under all circumstances, and it endures everything [without weakening].   *1 Corinthians 13:7*

Positive people who think positive thoughts and speak positive words have a much more enjoyable life than those who don't. Why are we so inclined to talk about negative things, or what God calls "evil things"? It is simply because human beings not controlled and guided by God's Spirit will always drift to the negative side of thinking. Oddly enough, we don't have to try to be negative or do what is wrong, but we do have to make an effort to do what is right. Especially until we form new habits. I don't have to try nearly as hard now to find the good in things as I once did, but I still have to exercise discipline in this area, especially when something happens that really hurts me.

I was unaware that I was a negative-thinking and -speaking person until God revealed it to me. I was raised in a very negative atmosphere; and therefore, being negative seemed normal to me. My father actually said to me many times, "You can't trust anybody, everybody is out to get something." I grew up being suspicious and just watching for what was wrong with people and life in general. I might add that doing so did not increase my joy.

As I began to study God's Word, I realized that some- thing was wrong. I almost always sensed a threatening feeling around me, a feeling of oppression, suggesting that something bad was going to happen. I was accustomed to being disappointed and having bad things happen, so I grew to expect nothing else. God doesn't want us to do that, but instead He wants us to aggressively look for and expect good things. His plan for us is a good plan, and we must agree with Him if we want to have His will manifested in our lives.

God taught me through His Word that I had what the Bible calls "evil forebodings."

All the days of the desponding and afflicted are made evil [by anxious thoughts and forebodings], but he who has a glad heart has a continual feast [regardless of circumstances].   *Proverbs 15:15*

Do you perhaps have a case of "evil forebodings," or do you know someone who does? It is a terrible thing to endure because everything in life seems dark and dreary. A person with evil forebodings always expects the worst. The night that Dave asked me to marry him, he told me he wanted to talk to me about something serious and I immediately thought he was going to tell me he didn't want to date me any longer. In those days, that was just the way my mind worked. After Dave and I had been married about three weeks, he looked at me one day and said, "What is wrong with you? Why are you so negative about everything?" I answered, "If you don't expect anything good to happen, then you won't be disappointed when it doesn't." As you can see, I had a serious problem, and Dave, who was very positive about everything, ended up being a great example for me.

I was thrilled when I realized that God wanted me to renew my thinking and start expecting good things. Surely we would all prefer good things more than bad ones. Even if you have had a sad past, you can have a bright future by learning how to agree mentally and verbally with God. The change in me took a long time, and many times I felt as if I was making no progress at all, but as I continued studying and purposely looking for the good in everything and everyone, I changed. Now I actually cannot endure being negative or being around anyone negative for very long. I want you to be assured that negative thoughts and words can be exchanged for positive ones. The more positive we are, the more we enjoy our lives and the people in it. People also enjoy us more when we think and speak no evil. More good things will happen to people who expect them than to those who don't.

Bad News Travels Fast

It continues to amaze me how fast bad news travels. Something bad can happen in ministry circles all the way on the other side of the world and within twenty-four hours everyone knows about it. At least they know some version of it. One of the worst things about spreading bad news is that people keep adding to it and changing the context of what originally happened until eventually the stories being told are not the truth at all. This is one of the reasons why we need to be very careful about believing everything we hear. God's Word teaches us not to believe an accusation against anyone unless we have confirmation from several people. We are too quick to give bad reports and often too quick to believe them.

I realize that we have a lot of unpleasant situations in our society today, but I still believe there is more good than bad. The problem is that we don't hear about the good as much as we do the bad. The media consistently reports bad news and even sensationalizes it, and it sounds worse than it actually is. I know firsthand because I have been the subject of their reporting at times, and I can assure you that what was reported was far from the truth. The world would be a better place if our first response to unfounded rumors and gossip would be, "I don't believe that." Sometimes what we hear ends up being true, but it should be proven to us before we jump on board with all the other people who are spreading bad news.

How Many Negative People Are in the World?

Sadly, I think there are more negative people in the world than those who are committed to finding the good in everyone and everything, but it can change, beginning with you and me. People who love God must fight for what is right and good, because if we don't, nobody else will. When godly people do nothing, evil increases. We should start a "believing the best" club. Even if the club consists only of your closest family members, just think what a difference it could make in everyone's attitude at home. Our mind and mouth will be tempted to drift toward the negative, but our free will is the big boss. When we begin using our will to take authority over all negativity, it will leave!

It isn't enough to merely "wish" that someone could become a more positive person. I know, because I tried it and nothing happened. I thought it was just my nature to be more suspicious, so I "wished" I had a different nature. I had to give up that excuse when I learned from scripture that God gives us a new nature when we receive Jesus as our Savior (see 2 Corinthians 5:17). I did have a new nature and so do you if you are a true believer in Jesus Christ. I wished I had a personality like Dave's, but I didn't get a personality transplant. I had to work with the Holy Spirit and allow Him to change the negative traits in me. All change begins by facing truth and not making any excuses for wrong behavior. The raw truth was that I had a negative attitude, and changing it was hard work, but it definitely was worth it in the end.

I said that we "drift" toward the negative if we don't use discipline and self-control. Everything in water will drift downstream if there is nothing propelling it upstream. Don't just drift into the negative parts of life, but instead push against them and find the good in everything.

Moses sent twelve men into the land of Canaan as spies to see if it was actually as good as God had told them it would be. When they returned from searching out the land, ten men gave a negative (evil) report. They said the fruit was good, but there were giants in the land and they were mightier than the Israelites. Only two men, Joshua and Caleb, gave a good report. They said, "We should not delay in taking the land for we are able to do it." The ten negative men saw only what was wrong. Admittedly there were giants and they were terrifying, but the two positive men saw God as bigger than any of the adverse circumstances. They looked for what was good! They gave a good report even though there were bad things they could have said. They focused on the good, and God said that they had a different spirit than the rest of the people (see Numbers 13:27–33). Their positive spirit was one that He approved of, and they were given the privilege of going into the land that God had promised.

Many of the children of Israel could not enter the good land, because they refused to see anything good. Truthfully, most of the people never entered into what God had prepared for them. If we look at these twelve spies as an example, then it looks like more people are negative rather than positive. But no matter how many negative people there are around us, if we persist in being positive, we will enjoy the good life God wants us to have. When we magnify something, we make it larger, so why not start magnifying the good things in life and help them stand out above evil things. Talk about the good in life, give the good report as the Bible teaches us to do, think about good things, and be good to other people.

Start at Home

Begin with yourself and make a list of all your good qualities. I know it may be hard for some of you, but you need to begin seeing the good traits that you have and not just the bad ones. Satan reminds all of us daily what is wrong with us, but we can remind him what is right with us if we are bold enough to do so.

> That the communication of thy faith may become effectual by the acknowledging of every good thing which is in you in Christ Jesus.   *Philemon 1:6 KJV*

According to this scripture, we should acknowledge the good things in us. When we do, it will give us confidence to do and be all that God desires.

The thoughts and attitudes that we have are the foundation for all that comes from us. If we have a negative attitude, it is usually rooted in negative thoughts about ourselves.

Start by having a right and godly attitude toward yourself and work out from there. God works from the inside out, not from the outside in. For years I mistakenly thought that if my circumstances were better, my attitude would be better. I thought the outside could change the inside, but God works in the opposite way. He gives us a new nature and a new heart, He puts His Spirit in us, and He desires that we work with His Holy Spirit until what He has put in us by His grace is worked out of us and into every facet of our lives.

> Work out (cultivate, carry out to the goal, and fully complete) your own salvation with reverence and awe and trembling (self-distrust, with serious caution, tenderness of conscience, watchfulness against temptation, timidly shrinking from whatever might offend God and discredit the name of Christ).
>
> [Not in your own strength] for it is God Who is all the while effectually at work in you.   *Philippians 2:12–13*

God's Spirit is in us, and His Spirit is definitely positive. We must let His Spirit do a thorough work in us, changing our thoughts and attitudes toward ourselves and working from that foundation outward until we can see all things and people the way God sees them. Even when we are doing our worst, God believes the best in regard to us and He works with us to bring the best out of us.

We can start by thinking and saying, "God loves me unconditionally. He has given me His Spirit, and put a new heart and attitude in me. Everything in my spirit is good and positive and full of faith, and I will not allow the things that go on around me to dictate my attitude." Anytime we do anything that is sinful, we should immediately ask God to forgive us and go in a new direction. We should not ignore the wrong things that we do, but we should see and celebrate what we do that is *right*.

Perhaps you got your feelings hurt yesterday, but you quickly made the decision not to be offended and let it go. That is a good thing! Maybe you had plans for your day, but a friend needed help and you changed your plans to help your friend. That is a good thing! If you spent time with God this morning in prayer and fellowship and you studied His Word, then that is a good thing! I am sure there are many good things in you and you should begin to recognize them.

The more positive you are about yourself, the more positive you will be about other people and your circumstances. Believe the best of yourself and all the people that you deal with.

12

Speak Faith, Not Fear

Be careful of your thoughts; they may
become words at any moment.
—Ira Gassen

The Word of God teaches us to hold fast our confession of faith in Jesus Christ (see Hebrews 4:14). That means that no matter what our situation in life feels or looks like, we should continue to speak faith, not fear. That doesn't mean that we deny our circumstances, but we do deny them the right to rule over us.

If we believe that words have power, then we can easily understand why it is very important for us to maintain a confession of faith in Jesus Christ in all circumstances. When Jesus stood in front of the tomb of Lazarus, intending to raise him from death, Martha spoke out of her fears. She said, "But Lord, by this time he [is decaying and] throws off an offensive odor, for he has been dead four days!" (John 11:39). Jesus responded by saying, "Did I not tell you and promise you that if you would believe and rely on Me, you would see the glory of God" (John 11:40).

I rely on that scripture when I don't understand anything that is going on around me. Even when my circumstances in life are so painful they seem unbearable, I try to remember to say, "I believe and I will see the glory of God."

The word *glory* means the "manifestation of God's excellence." Seeing the glory of God does not necessarily mean that we get things the way we want them all the time. But it does mean that we can trust God for His best in every situation. It may not seem best to us at the time, but we should trust God that His plan is better than ours. We would like to understand everything that God does, but trusting God means that we will always have some unanswered questions, and we must accept that. We don't have to understand all of God's ways to say, "I believe God, and I will see His glory."

Fear Comes

Fear comes to every person. It seems to be the first emotion we feel when things in our lives get beyond our control. When the surrounding armies came against Jehoshaphat, he feared (see 2 Chronicles 20:3). But then he prayed. Resist the devil at his onset—don't allow fear to get embedded in your thinking and start coming out of your mouth.

Jehoshaphat felt fear, but he spoke faith, and we can do the same thing. In the Garden of Gethsemane, Jesus felt such intense agony that He sweated drops of blood and He asked that, if possible, God would remove the cup of suffering from Him, and yet He was crucified for our sins. When He hung upon the cross in unbelievable agony, feeling the crushing weight of the sins of the world upon Him, and feeling that His Father had forsaken Him, He didn't say, "I am so afraid of what will happen to Me." He still prayed in faith and said, "Father, into your hands do I commit my Spirit." He held fast His confession of faith, and we can do the same thing.

In 1989, I went to the doctor for a regular checkup. Within a few days I was told that I had breast cancer on the right side and radical surgery was indicated owing to the type of cancer it was. I can tell you for sure that "fear came." Fear was the first emotion that I felt, and it was so overwhelming at times that I actually felt that my knees would buckle underneath me. The Holy Spirit whispered in my heart that it was important for me to speak faith and not fear. I had a lot of time to practice while I waited for surgery and then for reports to come back letting me know if the cancer was successfully eradicated. Satan tries to take advantage of our times of waiting, and he bombards our minds with fearful thoughts. I don't have any secret to tell you that will keep the fearful thoughts from coming, but I do know that you don't have to receive them as your own, and speak them out of your mouth. Your mouth and your words belong to you, and you can always choose to speak what will please God and benefit you.

The apostle Matthew wrote, "Do not worry and be anxious, saying, What are we going to have to eat? or, What are we going to have to drink? or, What are we going to have to wear?" (Matthew 6:31). Notice that the worry comes first and then the saying. It is the same with fear—first the thoughts and then the words. I would like to suggest something to you that I try to practice myself. As soon as a fearful thought enters my mind, I speak out loud if I am in an appropriate place, saying, "I will not fear, I trust God." Or I say, "I believe God and I will see His glory." If I cannot speak out loud, I combat the evil thought by thinking faith thoughts. If I have something intense going on in my circumstances, there are days when it seems like I battle all day, but we must be willing to fight the good fight of faith.

I did have to stand firm during the weeks I waited for all the tests to come back, but the reports were all good and I needed no further treatment at all. Many years have gone by since then, and each year I get tested and am told, "No cancer!" That challenge is over, but new ones arise on a regular basis, as they do for everyone.

Even as I write this book, there are things taking place around me that would love to distract and frighten me, but I am still saying, "I believe God and I will see His glory."

If you are dealing with an unpleasant situation in your life right now, stop reading and say out loud about five times, "I believe God and I will see His Glory."

I keep a sign sitting in front of me on a table where I pray and study that simply says in big sparkly letters: BELIEVE. It reminds me to continue believing in God's promises anytime doubt or fear tries to come in. Quite often I verbalize my faith and declare it out loud! In my office all by myself I declare that I believe God!

The psalmist David said, "What time I am afraid, I will trust in You, Lord." He admitted that he felt fear, but declared that he would trust God in the midst of it. I have heard that there are 365 references in God's Word that say "fear not," and that is one for every day of the year. "Fear not" means to resist fear and don't let it control your actions. We can act in faith while we still feel fear. The only acceptable attitude that God's children can ever have toward fear is: "I will not fear." If you let fear rule in your life, it will steal your peace and joy and prevent you from fulfilling your destiny.

The Lord is on my side; I will not fear. What can man do to me?   *Psalm 118:6*

If we enter into fear and begin to speak it, it is equivalent to having faith in what the devil says to us or shows us in our imaginations. We can steadfastly resist him, but we must know the Word of God, and form a habit of aggressively talking back to the devil! When he says something to you, you should say something to him. Anytime doubt, worry, or fear comes, instead of saying, "I am afraid," or "I am worried," or "I doubt," say, "I believe God and I will see His glory," or quote another scripture that you feel fits the situation you are in.

Make "I will not fear" a daily confession in your life. Don't wait until you feel fear, but confess daily that you are bold and fearless. Be prepared ahead of time, and it will help you be more than a conqueror when adverse situations arise. I believe we are more than conquerors, as Romans 8 says we can be, when we know we will win the battle before it ever begins. Are you that confident in God? Do you believe right now that no matter what comes against you, you are assured of victory through Christ? I recommend that you form a habit of saying, "I will not fear," several times a day. If you do, then it will be one of the first things that come out of your mouth when fear does come.

Let the Redeemed of the Lord Say So!

What do you say about yourself and your life? I hear people say things that make me want to cringe at times, but I once talked the same way they do. I hear things like, "I am a failure," "I am really in bondage to food," "I wish I was free from fear," "I am going to give up," or "My problems are overwhelming." They are saying what they think and how they feel, but it doesn't agree with God's Word.

> Let the redeemed of the Lord say so, whom He has delivered from the hand of the adversary.   *Psalm 107:2*

The Bible says that those who belong to God are redeemed and they should say so. We are redeemed! We are not waiting to be redeemed because Jesus has already paid the price for our redemption. It is ours, and we need to learn to agree with it. The person who has a problem with food should not say, "I am in bondage to food," but he should say, "I have discipline and self-control, and I eat what is good for me in quantities that are right for my body." If he continues saying he is in bondage, he will continue believing he is, but if he agrees with God and says that he is free, he will act accordingly. One should never say, "I wish I were free from fear," as if it were something floating around that we might catch if we wish hard enough. She should say, "I will not fear, I am bold, and I am free from fear." Or instead of saying, "My problems are overwhelming me," she should say, "I can do whatever I need to do in life, through Christ, Who is my strength."

If we truly live by faith and believe the promises of God, then our confession must change. We must hold fast our confession of faith in God regardless of what we think, how we feel, or how things look. Faith is the evidence of things hoped for, the proof of things we do not see (see Hebrews 11:1). We make a confession of faith because we believe God's Word, not because we see or feel a certain thing.

The apostle Paul wrote to the Church in Rome, "How can we live in sin any longer, since we are dead to sin?" (see Romans 6:2). I don't know many Christians who would say they are dead to sin, because that is not how they feel. Paul wanted people to live in the reality of their redemption, which Jesus accomplished on the cross. He wanted them to believe and say they were redeemed according to God's Word.

"Let the redeemed of the Lord say so!" Start declaring by faith, "I am redeemed from sin, guilt, and condemnation. I am redeemed from anger, bitterness, jealousy, fear, and I am free to love God, love myself, and love other people." We must get these truths into our spirit before we will have them in our experience. Faith comes first, and then mani-festation comes. In God's kingdom, first we believe and then we receive. I said, "God loves me," thousands of times by faith before I ever felt it. We might say that confession is a large part of possession. We choose to believe what

God says and say the same thing by faith. The result is that our confession of God's promises leads us to possess them experientially.

God's principle of faith is the exact opposite of what the world teaches. It would say, "Don't believe anything that you can't see, smell, or touch." God says that we walk by faith, not by sight!

Let the redeemed of the Lord say so! When we have had the privilege of learning God's Word, we should speak His Word faithfully according to the prophet Jeremiah.

> The prophet who has a dream, let him tell his dream; but he who has My word; let him speak My word faithfully.   *Jeremiah 23:28*

God is faithful, and that means we can expect Him to do what He says He will do all the time. He doesn't do it part of the time, but all the time, and every time. There is never a time when God doesn't keep His promises. We should also be faithful to do what we know to do all the time. Saying the right thing occasionally won't give us victory. But when we are relentless and we speak the word faithfully, then we will see amazing results in due time.

Don't merely do what is right for a short while and then give up if you don't get a quick result. Do what is right over and over until you break the strongholds of Satan. The Bible says that we have weapons that we can use to tear down strongholds (see 2 Corinthians 10:4–5). I believe the main one is the Word of God spoken in faith. The Word may be taught, preached, read, sung, or spoken, and it is only the Word of God that will tear down demonic strongholds that have been erected in our minds through deception. The truth demolishes the lies of Satan!

Get Rid of the Mixture

We need to be faithful to the principles of God. Don't think you can have a little faith and a little fear and still come out victorious. We can't speak the Word some of the time, but speak doubt and unbelief as well and hope for a good result. If we do that, the bad cancels out the good and we end up back with "no power."

When I started learning these principles, I disciplined myself to speak positively when I was with my friends from church, but at home I reverted to my same old negative self, speaking words of fear, worry, and doubt. As you might imagine, I experienced no change in my joy or breakthrough in my circumstances. I needed to get rid of the mixture of positive and negative, of faith and fear words, and be committed to doing the right thing all the time. I knew the right thing to do, but I let my emotions rule at times, and I needed to be much more serious about the words I spoke.

I still make mistakes, but I no longer take a light attitude toward negative words and think that they are no big deal. Words are a big deal. They are containers for power, and we have to decide what kind of power we want ours to carry.

Keep pressing on and pressing toward improving in every

area of your life, especially in speaking faith, not fear, and maintaining a confession that will glorify God.

Fear Is Not from God

Timothy was a very young man who lived in a time when Christians were being persecuted. He was the apostle Paul's spiritual son and had been ordained for the Gospel ministry by the elders, but fear was attacking him. He was concerned that he was too young for ministry, and that he would be persecuted for his belief in Jesus. Paul told him to stir up his faith, to fan the flame and not let the fire that was once in him go out. The longer we allow fearful thoughts, the more tightly they grip us. If we talk about our fears, we fan the flame of fear. But if we talk about God's goodness, His faithfulness to us in the past, and the privilege of living by faith, we fan the flame of our faith and it stays alive and powerful. We don't automatically stay strong in faith, and there are times when we must stir ourselves up in faith and remind ourselves that we don't have to live in fear.

I am sure Timothy was doing too much negative thinking and had forgotten the rich heritage of faith he had received from his grandmother and mother, so Paul reminded him (see 2 Timothy 1:1–6). Sometimes we need someone to interrupt our negative talk and help us get back on track, and sometimes we need to lovingly remind others of the power of their words. We cannot take it upon ourselves to correct the mistakes of others all the time, but we can and should be led by the Holy Spirit to speak a word in due season to those who have an open heart, as Paul did to Timothy.

Paul finally told Timothy:

God did not give us a spirit of timidity (of cowardice, of craven and cringing and fawning fear), but [He has given us a spirit] of power and of love and of calm and well-balanced mind and discipline and self-control.   *2 Timothy 1:7*

Fear is not from God; therefore, the next time you feel fear, open your mouth and say, "This fear is not from God, and I don't believe it and won't receive it." Then say boldly, "I believe God and I will see His glory." It might help to remember what FEAR stands for:

F—False
E—Evidence
A—Appearing
R—Real

Satan attempts to frighten us with his lies, but thank God we don't have to live in fear!

PART II

The second part of this book consists of chapters about things that are good to say and things that we should not say. I want to encourage you to purposely say things that would please God, even though you may feel like saying something that would not please Him. I also want to encourage you *not* to say things that would not please God. Say things that will help and benefit you and the people you interact with, and avoid saying things that won't help or bring benefit. This is a super simple guideline to how to have a more powerful and joy-filled life.

Now that you know the power of words, you are more likely to discipline yourself to say right things that are pleasing to God.

God has given us a free will, and with His help, we can choose to say what we know is right in any situation even if we feel like saying something that would be merely emotional and damaging to others or ourselves. I want to discuss some of what I refer to as the most common "word sins." These are words we speak that are useless and or even damaging. They are things that are not pleasing to God, and in most instances things He has commanded us in His Word not to say. Most people don't consider sins of this type as being very important. At least not as important as the "bigger sins," such as adultery, stealing, lying, or murder, but they are more important than most of us realize. We may categorize sin as big and little, but I don't think God does. Some sins may have a greater impact on our lives than others, but sin is sin, and it is all disobedience to God. Let us desire to obey God in all things, all the time!

Quite often we open a door for big problems in our lives through things we say, but when we cooperate with God's plan by saying what He would say in every situation, we avoid many painful traps that Satan has laid for us.

As I said earlier, please remember that it is important not only to stop saying wrong things, but *to begin saying right things*. Words are containers for power, and we can decide what kind of power we want to fill them with. We can complain or be thankful, we can encourage or discourage others, we can bless or curse our own future, and we can open or close doors of opportunity by the way we speak to others. It is time to use wisdom with what we say. Let us be able to say with David:

> I will speak excellent and princely things; and the opening of my lips shall be for right things.
> For my mouth shall utter truth, and wrongdoing is detestable and loathsome to my lips.
> All the words of my mouth are righteous (upright and in right standing with God); there is nothing contrary to truth or crooked in them.   *Proverbs 8:6–8*

CHAPTER 13

Don't Complain

> *To complain of the age we live in, to murmur at the*
> *present possessors of power, to lament the past... are the*
> *common dispositions of the greatest part of mankind.*
> —Edmund Burke, 1770

Are You a Duck or an Eagle?

A taxi driver picked up an airport customer in New York City and immediately introduced himself as Wally. He offered his passenger a cold drink from a cooler in the front seat, that day's newspaper, and his choice of music from a few well-chosen CDs. The client was amazed and asked, "Have you always served your customers like this?"

Wally said, "No, not always. My first five years of driving, I spent complaining like all the rest of the cabbies do. Then I heard a motivational speaker on the radio one day. He said that if you wake up expecting to have a bad day, you'll rarely disappoint yourself. Then he said, 'Stop complaining! Don't be a duck. Be an eagle. Ducks quack and complain. Eagles soar above the crowd.' That day I decided to stop quacking like ducks and start soaring like eagles."

I want you to do an experiment with me. Just as an exercise, take a day or two and purposely listen to how much people complain, and while you are at it, don't forget to also listen to yourself. I think making it through one day without complaining about anything would qualify as a miraculous occurrence.

Because our mouth gives expression to what we think and feel, it reveals our heart's attitude toward most things. We can judge by our words if we are thankful and appreciative of God's goodness, or if we are discontent. If we are discontent, then believe it or not, we have an underlying attitude of greed. Greedy people are never satisfied for long, no matter what they have or experience, and greed is a sin.

Murmuring, grumbling, and complaining are all what I will refer to as "word sins." They are sins that we commit with the words of our mouths, but they are also revealing a deeper problem, and that is a heart that is not thankful.

When I am teaching on this subject, I often ask people to open their Bibles to Philippians 2:14 and read it. It's never long before I hear moans, groans, and guilty laughter all across the room. The verse says, "Do all things without grumbling and faultfinding and complaining [against God] and questioning and doubting [among yourselves]." People are immediately convicted of wrongdoing when they read this verse because it is something that most of us do on a daily, if not an hourly, basis. You might think, "I don't complain against God, I just complain," but God takes it personally. Since He is our Father, our Provider, and the One Who watches over us, when we complain about anything, we are basically saying that we don't like what God is doing, and we don't trust His leadership in our lives. Even if what is happening in our circumstances is not something God is doing, it is something that He can fix if we will trust Him to do so. If we truly trust God, then we won't murmur and complain, but instead we will voice our thankfulness that He is working in our lives and giving us the strength to do whatever we need to do while we are waiting.

Are You Passing Your Tests?

Let's say, for example, that you are praying for God to help you get a pay raise at work, but instead you have to take a pay cut because of economic conditions. What would you say about that? Would you immediately start complaining, or would you say, "God, I trust You to take care of me, and if my current employer cannot or will not pay me what I am worth and need to live on properly, then I ask You to lead me to another position that will."

What would you say if in the upcoming days you discovered that not everyone had to take a cut in pay and that, in fact, some who you think were less deserving even received a small cost-of-living raise? Would you complain louder and even add words of criticism toward other people who didn't have to take a cut in pay? Or would you continue to voice your trust in God and thank Him that He is working in your life? Just because something doesn't seem just or fair doesn't mean that we have a free pass from God to complain about it. There are many things in life that are not fair, but God is our Vindicator, and He will eventually bring justice if we continue to trust Him. It is entirely possible that a situation like the one I have described is a test from God and that He fully intends to greatly bless the one who apparently is being treated unjustly, if he or she passes the test. We must praise and bless God in the valleys of life as well as on the mountaintops.

God told the Israelites that He led them through the wilderness in order to see if they would keep His commandments or not (see Deuteronomy 8). If you are in a difficult or trying situation right now, discipline yourself not to complain, but instead give praise and glory to God.

As I said, God sometimes allows us to be in less than desirable situations to test us. Quite often He is planning a promotion for us in life if we pass the test that is in front of us. I won't share the details of the situation, but I will tell you that even as I write this chapter, I am experiencing a situation in my own life that is quite unfair and unjust and one that I am tempted to complain about often. I am glad to be writing this chapter if for no one else, then for myself, because I need it. I am being tested right now. Are you?

Beloved, do not be amazed and bewildered at the fiery ordeal which is taking place to test your quality, as though something strange (unusual and alien to you and your position) were befalling you.   *1 Peter 4:12*

We are like children in school who must pass tests in order to be promoted to the next grade. Are you passing the trust test, or merely murmuring when things don't go your way? I am asking this because God has posed this very question to me in my personal life many times. God has dealt quite firmly with me about the issue of complaining and continues to do so. Complaining is a sin, and we must not look at it any other way.

Our prayers of petition have no power with God unless they are immersed in prayers of thanksgiving. God's Word teaches us not to worry about anything, but in every circumstance by prayer and petition, *WITH THANKSGIVING* (emphasis mine), continue to make your wants known to God (see Philippians 4:6).

Wisdom tells us that offering a prayer of petition to God with complaining would have no power. Such a prayer would have no chance of being answered. We cannot even come into the presence of God unless we come with thanksgiving.

Enter into His gates with thanksgiving and a thank offering and into His courts with praise! Be thankful and say so to Him, bless and affectionately praise His name! *Psalm 100:4*

A lot of prayers are wasted words because they are coming from the mouth of a person who murmurs, complains, and finds fault with many things. God does not answer prayers for this type of person because he is showing by his attitude and words that he does not trust God and is not thankful and appreciative. Don't make the mistake of thinking that your case is special and therefore your complaining is justified. We can all find many reasons to complain, but I have not found one reason that is acceptable to God.

You may be a person who genuinely loves God, but you have a habit of complaining and have not, until now, realized how disrespectful it is to God. That was the case with me. I had a bad habit of complaining, and an attitude problem. Bad habits usually come from bad attitudes, and we will never change until we receive the truth and let it set us free. It is not easy to admit that we have a bad attitude, but it is the road to freedom and change.

Are you thankful? Do you voice your thankfulness to God and others? How much do you murmur and complain? If you are convicted of sin in this area, there is no condemnation, but you should ask God to forgive you and learn all you can about what God has to say about the dangers of complaining.

Is It Really a Sin to Complain?

The Israelites were slaves in Egypt and they cried to God for deliverance for many years. God did send them a deliverer. He sent Moses, whom He had equipped to lead them out of Egypt, through the wilderness, and into the land He had promised to give them, a land of abundance where they would be blessed in many ways.

The journey from Egypt to the land of Canaan that God had promised to give them was an eleven-day trip, but they wandered in the wilderness for forty years. The majority of them died in the wilderness and never saw the reality of God's promise. Like most of us do, they blamed their lack of progress on many things. It was God's fault, Moses' fault, and all the enemy nations that surrounded them. Oddly enough, they never thought or even considered that it was their own fault. Does that sound familiar?

They remained in the wilderness because they had a bad attitude, and one of their sins was the sin of murmuring, faultfinding, and complaining.

> And they journeyed from Mount Hor by the way to the Red Sea, to go around the land of Edom, and the people became impatient (depressed, much discouraged), because [of the trials] of the way.   *Numbers 21:4*

Like many of us, the Israelites were satisfied, content, and thankful only when everything was going their way, but when there were trials, they complained.

> And the people spoke against God and against Moses, Why have you brought us out of Egypt to die in the wilderness? For there is no bread, neither is there any water, and we loathe this light (contemptible, unsubstantial) manna.   *Numbers 21:5*

Do you hear their bad attitude as you read this? Their discomfort is God's fault! It is Moses' fault! They are thinking about death instead of making progress! And worst of all, they are complaining about the miraculous manna that God has sent from heaven daily to feed them! One of the worst parts about complaining is that it prevents us from seeing all the blessings that we do have. The Israelites were once very excited about the manna (heavenly bread), but now they hate it. Their greedy attitude demands more and more.

Their greed and bad attitude blinded them to the goodness of God. When we allow ourselves to fall prey to this kind of bad attitude, it keeps us in the very circumstance that we want to get out of. I once saw a definition of the word *complain* that said it meant "to remain." When I complain about a situation, I remain in it, but an attitude of gratitude and praise will raise me out of it. The Israelites could not do anything but go around and around the same mountains, wandering in the desert, even though the border of the Promised Land was a few days away, simply because they murmured, blamed, and complained.

Do you have a situation or circumstance that you want to be free from? If so, then start finding things to be thankful for. Don't merely look at the things you don't have, but look at all you do have. Be thankful and say so! Your words of gratitude defeat the devil and thwart his plans for evil, but words of complaint help him accomplish his wicked plan. The Israelites murmured and complained and the Lord sent fiery burning serpents into their camp.

> Then the Lord sent fiery (burning) serpents among the people; and they bit the people, and many Israelites died.
>
> And the people came to Moses, and said, We have sinned, for we have spoken against the Lord and against you; pray to the Lord, that He may take away the serpents from us. So Moses prayed for the people.
> *Numbers 21:6–7*

It is a shame that people had to die before they realized that their bad attitude and harsh words were sin. A reference is made to these scriptures in 1 Corinthians 10:8 that tells us that twenty-three thousand Israelites fell dead that day. It was a tragic day, and it could have been avoided if the people would have simply trusted God and been thankful for what they had.

I am not saying that if we complain, we will drop dead, but I do believe there is a lesson in these scriptures that we don't want to miss. I am grateful that we live in the dispensation of grace and that God is merciful, but that still doesn't mean that we don't harm ourselves and hinder the plan of God for our lives when we continue murmuring and complaining even after understanding that it is a sin.

I ask that you take the time to read the next four verses and ponder them slowly. I know we are sometimes tempted to skip over the scriptures when we are reading books like this one, but please don't do that because these verses contain a solemn warning that we should pay heed to.

We must not gratify evil desire and indulge in immorality as some of them did—and twenty-three thousand [suddenly] fell dead in a single day!

We should not tempt the Lord [try His patience, become a trial to Him, critically appraise Him, and exploit His goodness] as some of them did and were killed by poisonous serpents;

Nor discontentedly complain as some of them did—and were put out of the way entirely by the destroyer (death).

Now these things befell them by way of a figure [as an example and warning to us]; they were written to admonish and fit us for right action by good instruction.
1 Corinthians 10:8–11

If you did what I asked and really took a good look at these verses, you are probably sitting with your mouth hanging open in amazement as I did the first time I simply believed what God is saying here. To sum it up, He is saying that the Israelites murmured and complained, and then instead of taking responsibility for their bad attitude, they further sinned by blaming God and Moses for the problems they had created themselves. Their disobedience opened a door for poisonous serpents (representing the devil) to attack them, and many of them died. Those who died were probably the ones who complained the loudest and poisoned other people's attitude with theirs. I am sure they knew better and understood the power of praise and thanksgiving, but they did not discipline themselves to honor God. The final verse plainly states that this was written down for our instruction and to help us not make the same mistakes they did.

Many years ago I decided to take these verses at face value, and I began at that time making an effort to stop complaining. I have not arrived at perfection. As a matter of fact, I recently realized that I complain almost daily about a three-mile stretch of highway close to my home that has no cell tower and I can't make phone calls during those three miles. The rest of the highway is fine, but I complain about the inconvenience of the three miles. I remember when I was a teenager and the only way to make a phone call if I was driving was to pull over in an area that had an outside phone booth, find the right change, and get out of my car to make the call. What we have available today is extremely convenient, but I complained about the short distance that probably takes three or four minutes to drive through. I asked

God to forgive me and to make me aware of it when I am complaining.

Now that I see what I was doing, it seems so utterly ridiculous, but it does show how we fall into the trap of complaining without even being fully aware of it. We need God's help!

I hope and pray that our eyes will be opened and we will make a genuine effort to no longer complain and instead be very thankful for all the goodness of God in our lives.

Through Him, therefore, let us constantly and at all times offer up to God a sacrifice of praise, which is the fruit of lips that thankfully acknowledge and confess and glorify His name.   *Hebrews 13:15*

CHAPTER
14

Words of Encouragement

Nothing else can quite substitute for a few well-chosen, well-timed, sincere words of praise. They're absolutely free—and worth a fortune.
—Sam Walton

Words of encouragement are perhaps some of the most valuable words in the world. The late Walt Disney said that there are three kinds of people in the world. First there are "well-poisoners," who discourage you and stomp on your creativity and tell you what you can't do. Then there are "lawn-mowers," people who are well intentioned but self-absorbed. They tend to their own needs, mow their own lawns, and never leave their yards to help another person. Finally there are "life-enhancers," people who reach out to enrich the lives of others, to lift them up and inspire them. We need to be life-enhancers, and we need to surround ourselves with life-enhancers.

The word *encourage* is defined in *Vine's Dictionary of the Bible* as "to urge forward, to persuade, or to comfort." It also means to stimulate one to the discharge of the ordinary duties in life. We all need encouragement because there are times in life when we get weary and feel like giving up. Let me mention at least three times in life when we may need encouragement.

The first is when we are facing great challenges or difficulty of some kind. It may be a financial burden, sickness, or caring for an elderly parent. It could be the loss of a loved one, marital difficulty, or a child who has gone astray. During those times we often think and feel that we just cannot go on, but a word of encouragement from someone we love and respect, or even from a total stranger, can give us the courage we need to press on and see victory. A word of encouragement during a crisis is worth more than an hour of praise after victory.

When we encourage others, we let them borrow our courage. Here is an interesting story that I heard:

Stonewall Jackson (who became the famed general for the Confederacy in the Civil War) was a student at the military school at West Point. Even though he was brilliant, he encountered a tough season and a particularly bad day in his military training. He made an appointment with his superior to get counsel. In the appointment he confided to his aged superior that he was discouraged. The officer stood up and declared, "I understand that you are discouraged. Not to worry, son. Today you shall borrow my courage!"

If nobody had been willing to encourage Jackson at this point in his career, it is possible that he would not have gone on to be the great general that he was. We can help people along their way by encouraging them.

A second area where we need encouragement is when we have great new opportunity in front of us. At times the call to do something greater than we have ever done before seems overwhelming. We wonder if we are up to it or can do what will be required. When we are given the opportunity to do something that we have never done before, we may begin to feel afraid that we will fail. A word of encouragement can make the difference between success and failure. Just to have someone say, "I believe in you and I know you have got what it takes," can give the strength someone needs to keep going. Little children especially need to know without a shadow of a doubt that their parents believe in them. Who wouldn't want confidence like the little boy who said to his father, "Let's play darts, Dad. I'll throw and you say, 'Wonderful!' "

One day I felt that I should text a very well-known musician whom I occasionally talk to and simply say to her, "I am proud of you for holding on to your faith in an industry that I know can be challenging." Normally, I would not think she would need me to encourage her because she is not just a music star, she is a megastar, but her response was as follows: "You will never know how much your encouragement meant to me. To know that you are proud of me is wonderful."

I realized later that a lot of people didn't or still don't get from their natural parents the encouragement that they need, and receiving it from a spiritual mother or father can make up for that loss in their life. Tell your children, even your grown children, that you are proud of them and watch them light up and stand taller.

The third area where we often need encouragement is simply in living ordinary, everyday life with enthusiasm. It is easy to get bored with discharging the duties of ordinary life. We get up and go to bed, get up and go to bed, and in

between we tend to endless chores that seem to repeat themselves every day. I find that a lot of our life is dealing with
these types of things. We cannot always have something new
happening, or be getting ready for an exciting vacation. Since
most of life is ordinary, we need to be able to live it with joy
and appreciation.

Brighten Someone's Day

Speaking words of encouragement to people helps them. It
is like a bright spot in an otherwise plain day. I find that
compliments encourage people. Yesterday I was in a checkout
line at a store, and an elderly woman was working at the cash
register. I noticed that even though her skin was wrinkled
from age, it had a very nice sheen, and she had lovely rosy
checks. Her skin made her look soft and kind, so I told her
so. I could tell that my compliment surprised her, but she
liked it. If I watch closely, it seems that when I compliment
people, they seem to stand a bit taller than they were previously, and a little light comes into their eyes, and they always
smile! We can put smiles on people's faces every day.

Make a habit of complimenting people. Say something kind
and encouraging to everyone you meet, and people will always
be happy to see you coming. You will be happier also, for when
we make others happy, it always comes back on us. When you
brighten someone else's day, you brighten yours also. Remember in the earlier part of the book that I said we eat our words,
and this is another way of seeing that principle in action. The
better I make others feel, the better I feel myself. Don't feel

embarrassed about complimenting people you don't know. Just because we don't know someone does not mean that God can't use us to increase her joy and build her up.

Many people that we come into contact with while we are out and about in our daily life are living in darkness. They either have no relationship with Jesus, Who is the Light of the world, or they have dark secrets they are running from, or their circumstances are dark and painful. We can let the Holy Spirit work through us in fulfilling one portion of His ministry, which is to comfort and encourage.

If more husbands and wives would compliment each other and show appreciation, there would be a lot fewer divorces. When people do divorce, they often think and claim it is due to some huge problem in their life, but I think it is often because they have forgotten the simple kindnesses in life that they should be showing each other. And even if there were more serious problems, perhaps they would never have developed if each of them had been encouraging the other. Dave and I have been married forty-five years as I write this book, and we are still complimenting each other. It is very ordinary and human to discourage and find fault, but it is a godly trait to be an encourager.

More Encouragers, Please

Flatter me, and I may not believe you. Criticize me, and
I may not like you. Ignore me, and I may not forgive
you. Encourage me, and I will not forget you.
—William Arthur Ward

Words of encouragement build people up and strengthen them to be all they can be in life. They help people not to give up on their dreams, but to press on until they have victory. I am very thankful for the people who have encouraged me in life, but I must say that I wish there had been more of them.

Jean Nidetch, a homemaker desperate to lose weight, decided that she needed some support while she tried to lose more than fifty pounds. She invited six overweight friends to join her in dieting and to meet in her home weekly to talk about staying on it. Those meetings ultimately became Weight Watchers, which Nidetch established in 1963. Today, it has more than one million members who meet in twenty-four countries. When Nidetch was asked what the secret of her success was in helping people lose weight, she replied: "When I was a teenager, I would cross a park where I saw mothers gossiping while the toddlers sat on their swings with no one to push them. I'd give them a push. You know what happens when you push a kid on a swing? Pretty soon he's pumping, doing it himself. That's what my role in life is—I'm there to give others a push."

We all need encouragement, and I am no exception.

When God called me to teach His Word, most of the people I knew were critical and very discouraging. They told me what I could not do and why I couldn't do it, and they frequently reminded me of my lack of ability. According to them, I did not have the right personality, I was not the right sex because only men were Bible teachers back in those days, and they reminded me that I was a woman. They told me I didn't have the right credentials because I had not been to seminary and didn't have enough education. I can safely say that only Dave and a couple of friends gave me encouragement. I was asked to leave my church, and was no longer welcome in the same social circles we had once been part of. I would have loved to have been surrounded by encouraging people, and I am sure it would have made my journey much easier.

Let me say that Satan is the author of discouragement, and although these people were Christians, they ignorantly allowed Satan to use them to try to hinder a plan that God had for my life. Their personal opinions and wrong mind-sets got in the way of their being able to help me make my journey. We should be very careful about discouraging people just because they want to do something that has not been done before. Thomas Edison was greatly discouraged by many while he was searching for the electric lightbulb, but I am glad that he kept pressing on. Alexander Graham Bell was thought to be crazy for thinking that people's voices could be carried through air waves, but now we all carry cell phones and can communicate across continents in mere seconds.

It is not that we cannot survive without encouragement, but just imagine how much easier things would be if we had more encouragers in our lives.

Many of the world's great inventions came through people who had to resist believing the discouraging words spoken to them by others. Thankfully, they didn't give up, but how many others have given up because they had nobody to encourage them along the way? How many great things have we missed because we don't have enough "encouragers" in the world? Probably more than we can imagine.

Children need encouragement as much as they need food,

clothing, and shelter. Sean and Leigh Anne Tuohy, the real-life couple portrayed in the movie *The Blind Side*, share the following story in their book *In a Heartbeat*: There is a little-known congressional program that awards internships to young people who have aged out of the foster care system. These are kids who were never adopted, and are no longer eligible for state support.

A senator employed one such man as an intern. One morning the senator breezed in for a meeting and discovered that his intern was already in the office, reorganizing the entire mailroom. The senator said to the intern, "This is amazing—the mailroom has never looked so clean. You did a great job."

A few minutes later the senator saw that the intern had tears streaming down his face. [He] said, "Son, are you okay?"

"Yes," the intern answered quietly.

"Did I say something to offend you?"

"No, sir."

"Well, what's wrong?"

The young man said, "That's the first time in my life anyone's told me that I did something good."

Absolutely anyone can make a commitment to encourage other people. All we have to do is ask God to use us and begin to see people the way He does. He sees the good in people and the possibilities that exist, and we can train ourselves to do the same thing. Look for the positive and magnify it! Ask God to put things in your heart that you can speak to others that will encourage them. For example, if you look at someone who is wearing purple and the thought comes to you, "You really look great in that color," then why not open your mouth and say so? They can't read your mind, but a word in due season, or at just the right time, is wonderful.

Sometimes a single word can make all the difference. Robert Schuller tells a story about a banker who always tossed a coin in the cup of a legless beggar who sat on the street outside the bank. But unlike most people, the banker would always insist on getting one of the pencils the man had beside him. "You are a merchant," the banker would say, "and I always expect to receive good value from merchants I do business with." One day the legless man was not on the sidewalk. Time passed and the banker forgot about him, until he walked into a public building and there in the concessions stand sat the former beggar. He was obviously the owner of his own small business now. "I have always hoped you might come by someday," the man said. "You are largely responsible for me being here. You kept telling me that I was a 'merchant.' I started thinking of myself that way, instead of a beggar receiving gifts. I started selling pencils—lots of them. You gave me self-respect, caused me to look at myself differently."

> A man has joy in making an apt answer, and a word spoken at the right moment—how good it is!   *Proverbs 15:23*

Some people are gifted as encouragers, and it seems to come naturally for them. They are amazing people who make everyone feel good anytime they are around. I was not naturally gifted in that way, but I have trained myself to be that way. I have to work at it a little harder and perhaps you do, too, but we can do it. We may not all be naturally gifted encouragers, but we are all commanded by God to encourage others, and if that isn't enough, we are also commanded not to discourage them through faultfinding and criticism.

We can see how much importance the apostle Paul placed on encouraging one another by what he wrote to the Thessalonian Church. He was aware of the difficulty of the times they were living in and knew that many would give up and not finish their journey of faith if they had no encouragement.

Therefore encourage (admonish, exhort) one another and edify (strengthen and build up) one another, just as you are doing.   *1 Thessalonians 5:11*

Encourage the timid and fainthearted, help and give your support to the weak souls, [and] be very patient with everybody [always keeping your temper].   *1 Thessalonians 5:14b*

Let's remember to follow his advice.

The Holy Spirit Is an Encourager

God obviously knows how important encouragement is because He sent us a Divine Comforter and Encourager when He sent the Holy Spirit. Nobody is as good at encouraging as He is, and it is only because we have Him in our lives that we can be successful even when we have no human agent to encourage us. The Holy Spirit is the *Parakletos*, the Greek word for one who walks alongside us, giving aid, encouraging, building us up, edifying, and comforting us. Jesus said that when He went away, He would send another Comforter, and He sent the Holy Spirit.

According to scripture, God is the source of every comfort and encouragement. I believe He wants to work through people to provide this amazing ministry, but thankfully He sends us His Spirit even when people fail.

Blessed be the God and Father of our Lord Jesus Christ, the Father of sympathy (pity and mercy) and the God [Who is the Source] of every comfort (consolation and encouragement),

Who comforts (consoles and encourages) us in every trouble (calamity and affliction), so that we may also be able to comfort (console and encourage) those who are in any kind of trouble or distress, with the comfort (consolation and encouragement) with which we ourselves are comforted (consoled and encouraged) by God. *2 Corinthians 1:3–4*

In the early days of this ministry, even though I didn't have an abundance of encouragement from people, I did receive courage to go on from the Holy Spirit. I experienced His comfort and it helped me develop a relationship of intimacy with Him! Don't despair if you don't get from people what you need, but instead go to God and He will always be more than enough in every situation. In fact, I believe there are times when God will not allow people to meet our needs simply because He wants to minister to us Himself.

God comforts us in our time of need so we might then comfort others in theirs. God always expects us to give away what He gives us. This is a spiritual law and is the way to keep a steady flow of whatever we need coming into our lives. God first gives to us and His Word says we are to give and it will be given unto us in an overflowing abundance (see Luke 6:38). We can never outgive God. The more we encourage others, the more encouraged we will be ourselves. If we merely receive God's comfort in our time of need, but then don't bother to encourage others, we will soon find that our fountain of comfort is no longer flowing when we need it. A harsh attitude toward other people closes the door to the mercy that we need ourselves.

Don't Let Your Own Problems Get in Your Way

Truly great people have the ability not to allow their own legitimate needs to stop them from being a blessing to others in need. Here is a story that makes my point:

Two men, both seriously ill, occupied the same hospital room. One man was allowed to sit up in his bed for an hour each afternoon to help drain fluid from his lungs. His bed was next to the room's only window. The other man had to spend all of his time flat on his back.

The men talked for hours on end. They spoke of their wives and families, their homes, their jobs, their involvement in the military service, where they had been on vacation. And every afternoon when the man in the bed by the window could sit up, he would pass the time by describing to his roommate all the things he could see outside the window.

The man in the other bed began to live for those one-hour periods where his world would be broadened and enlivened by all the activity and color of the world outside.

The window overlooked a park with a lovely lake. Ducks and swans played on the water while children sailed their model boats. Young lovers walked arm in arm amid flowers of every color of the rainbow. Grand old trees graced the landscape, and a fine view of the city skyline could be seen in the distance.

As the man by the window described all this in exquisite detail, the man on the other side of the room would close his eyes and imagine the picturesque scene. One warm afternoon the man by the window described a parade passing by. Although the other man couldn't hear the band, he could see it in his mind's eye as the gentleman by the window portrayed it with descriptive words.

Days and weeks passed. One morning, the day nurse arrived to bring water for their baths only to find the lifeless body of the man by the window, who had died peacefully in his sleep. She was saddened and called the hospital attendants to take the body away. As soon as it seemed appropriate, the other man asked if he could be moved next to the window. The nurse was happy to make the switch, and after making sure he was comfortable, she left him alone.

Slowly, painfully, he propped himself up on one elbow to take his first look at the world outside. Finally, he would have the joy of seeing it for himself. He strained to slowly turn to look out the window beside the bed. It faced a blank wall. The man asked the nurse what could have compelled his deceased roommate who had described such wonderful things outside this window. The nurse responded that the man was blind and could not even see the wall. She said, "Perhaps he just wanted to encourage you."

The blind man definitely fulfilled the scripture that reads:

Let each one of us make it a practice to please (make happy) his neighbor for his good and for his true welfare, to edify him [to strengthen him and build him up spiritually]. *Romans 15:2*

For anyone who is wondering what his purpose in life is, let him wonder no more. We cannot find a higher purpose than to join the Holy Spirit in His ministry of comfort and encouragement.

CHAPTER
15

Love Listens and Speaks

We can and should form the habit of loving people with our words, but before we can do that properly, we need to learn to truly listen to them. Hearing is not the same as listening, or at least we can say that true listening is a deeper level of hearing. Part of the definition of *hearing* in *Vine's Dictionary of the Bible* is "to listen and be listening or to hear through fully." We can see from this that just because we hear someone's voice, and even if we understand the words that are spoken, that doesn't mean that we are truly listening with a caring ear.

I will admit right now that this is an area in which I need to improve. I probably still like to talk more than I like to listen, but I am growing! I find that I get impatient with people who give me too many details when they tell me things. I just want the bottom line, but I still need to respectfully listen to others because we all communicate based on our own personalities. We need the people who have the detailed personalities because we would miss a lot in life and make many mistakes if those wonderful people did not exist. God places different gifts and abilities in each one of us, and we should learn to appreciate each individual and his or her uniqueness.

Dave is more detailed than I am, so when he tells me stories about things he has seen or heard, it takes him longer than it would take me to tell them. Some of the details that he likes to share may not seem important to me, but they are obviously important to him, and part of love is listening respectfully. So now that I have confessed my weakness, I will go on and we will see together what we can learn.

Active Listening

Jesus said that if we love Him, we will obey Him. But we cannot obey Him if we don't listen to what He wants to say to us. How we listen to Bible teaching determines what we get out of it. The Bible says that the measure of thought and study that we give to the truth that we hear is the measure of virtue and knowledge we will receive from it (see Mark 4:24).

We can hear what is being said without truly *hearing* what is being said. Most people cannot tell you what they heard in church four hours after they were there. They thought they listened, but it was only surface listening. It is good to take notes when you are hearing something that you don't want to forget. Think over what you heard; ponder it. The more you do, the more you glean from it. For example, I can hear a sermon on sacrificial love and how important it is that I sacrifice my own desires to help others, but what does that really mean? If I don't think about it, I may either misunderstand it, or not understand it enough to cause me to take any action at all. I sat in the building, I heard the words, but I did not really hear the message if it doesn't move me to action.

If I spend time thinking about it, I will realize that to sacrifice doesn't mean that it is wrong to do things for myself, or things that I enjoy. It does mean that I cannot live solely for myself and expect to always get my own way. To sacrifice for others means that there will be times when the Holy Spirit will prompt me to take my time and money that I had plans for and use them instead for the benefit of someone in need. In our Christian society, we are often educated way beyond our level of obedience, and I think it is because we don't listen deeply enough to what we hear. We hear the surface of what is being said, but not the depth. Therefore, even though we may hear the same thing over and over, it never changes our behavior.

I think we also listen to people that way when they talk to us, and that is why we often don't realize we are in the presence of a hurting and very needy person. Sadly, we heard the sound of their words, but we didn't really listen.

How often has a man or a woman tried to tell their marriage partner that they are unfulfilled, lonely, and unhappy, just to be ignored or to be told the way they feel is silly? Far too often, and then a bad situation gets worse, and the unhappy partner is tempted to get from someone else what they should be getting in the marriage. Ultimately the couple divorce, and many people get hurt. The partner who didn't listen shakes their head in disbelief saying, "I don't know what happened." But what happened may be that they failed to listen. Had they listened, they could have said, "Tell me more, because I want to know how you feel and I want to meet your legitimate needs."

Or perhaps an employer has told an employee that she is not satisfied with his work performance, or that his tardiness will not be tolerated long term, but the employee doesn't really listen. The employee heard the boss, but didn't take what she said seriously. Then he is shocked when he loses his job. I recall one man who lost his position at our ministry and said, "If you weren't satisfied with my performance, why didn't you let me know? I should have been warned I was in danger of losing my job." But we had talked to him several times, and it was even documented in his file at work. He heard, but he didn't really listen.

We should form a habit of truly listening. First and foremost, we should listen to God. If we do, it will save us a lot of trouble and embarrassment in life. I recall our son David saying a few years ago, "Mom and Dad, I can honestly say that every time you have to correct me about something at work or a bad attitude I am having, God has already tried to tell me several times what you have just told me. I will be glad when I learn to listen to Him, so I don't have to keep going through the pain and embarrassment of being corrected by you." I am sure we can all relate to that because we have had the same thing happen to us. If we listen to God, He will always lead us in the way that we should go. The Bible says that wisdom cries out in the streets, but no one listens.

We can love God by saying, "Yes, Lord," to all of His instructions, but first we must truly listen.

Listen to Yourself

Listening to ourselves can be quite an education. The Bible teaches us that what we say comes from our heart; therefore, we can learn a lot about the deeper things in us by listening. If we learn more about ourselves and are willing to face truth, then we can love ourselves enough to change. If you are willing to discipline yourself to change, you are showing love for yourself as well as God and other people. Disciplining yourself to be the best you can be is displaying a loving attitude toward yourself and it is a good thing. God wants us to love ourselves properly because we are His creation.

A. B. Simpson said in his book *The Gentle Love of the Holy Spirit*, "Temperance is true self-love, and the proper regard for our own real interests, which is as much the duty of love as is regard for the interests of others." I want to be sure you don't miss this beautiful point. Disciplining yourself to be all you can be is showing genuine love for yourself and it is just as important as showing love for other people.

If you hear yourself saying all the time that you are tired, then perhaps you should listen to yourself and get some rest. If you frequently hear yourself say that you are stressed because your schedule is too busy, then perhaps you should make healthy changes in your schedule. If we know what is wrong in our lives and we continue to ignore it, then we are not showing proper love for ourselves. I will be bold and say that if we don't love ourselves in a balanced way, then we really don't love God as completely as we should, because He commands it. We are to love Him first and then love our neighbor as we love ourselves. A good relationship with God, ourselves, and our fellowman is necessary to be in full obedience to God.

We should also form a habit of listening to what we say about ourselves. Don't make downgrading comments about yourself. Don't say things like, "I am stupid," or "I never do anything right," or "I am a failure." I was with someone recently who lost his wallet and he must have said ten times, "I am so stupid!" I kept saying, "No, you're not stupid, you just made a mistake." I recall being on the golf course with Dave and listening to a man in his group call himself an "idiot" every time he made a shot he didn't like. I thought, "I wish this man knew what damage he is doing to his self-image by his own words."

We are taught in God's Word not to think more highly of ourselves than we ought to, and not to think we are better than other people, but we are not taught to have a low opinion of ourselves either. Once again let me say we should value ourselves because we are created in God's own image. What you say about yourself is one of the most important issues in your life. I think I mentioned earlier that it has been scientifically proven that we believe more of what we hear ourselves say than what anyone else says to us, so be careful what you say to yourself, about yourself!

What Are People Really Saying When They Talk?

I am sure you have heard the statement "I tried to read between the lines." People say this when they have been talking to someone who they feel is trying to tell them something covertly. In other words, the person is not being straightforward, but she is hoping we will hear her anyway.

Most of us often ask others, "How are you today?" Sometimes it is just a polite habit, and we really don't even care how the person is. But if we do care, then we should learn to read between the lines. If I ask someone how she is and she responds in a weak voice, "Okay," she is really telling me that something is wrong. She is having a rough day, a rough year, or a rough life, and it is an opportunity for me to love her with my words. Because I have really listened, I can realize that this person is hurting in some way, and I can ask myself, "How can I encourage her?"

If I do that, it won't be long before God will drop something in my heart to ask or say that shows I care about her. As I said earlier, we don't even need to know people well to do this. I may say to a sales clerk or an employee, "I know you have been working here a long time and I want you to know that I've noticed you do a really good job," or "Thank you for helping me." This can make a huge difference for the person who is tired and weary.

Sometimes we ask people how they are and they are honest and tell us, but we don't want to take time to truly hear their sad story, so we say something that means nothing to them, and then run off to our next thing in life. Have you ever told someone how you really were when he asked and seen him cringe—or say, "That's too bad," and change the subject as soon as possible? Have you ever been the person at the other end of that exchange?

A successful businesswoman recently shared the story of

the most important lesson she ever learned in school. During an economics class, her professor told his students to put away their notebooks; he was giving them a "pop quiz." She was a good student and had breezed through the questions until she read the last one: "What is the first name of the woman who cleans the school?" Surely this was some kind of a joke, she thought.

She had seen the cleaning woman several times. She was tall, dark-haired, and in her fifties. But how would the student know her name? She handed in her paper, leaving the last question blank. Just before the class ended, one student asked if the last question would count toward the quiz grade. "Absolutely," said the professor. "In your careers, you will meet many people. All are significant. They deserve your attention and care, even if all you do is smile and say 'hello.'" The businesswoman says, "I've never forgotten that lesson. I also learned that her name was Dorothy."

Jesus stopped for people all the time. He had a schedule, a plan, and a purpose as we do, but He always had time for people, especially if they were hurting. He stopped for a blind man, a crippled man, the woman with the issue of blood, the mother whose son had died, an army officer whose servant was sick, the father whose daughter was dying, little children, and anyone else who had a need. When Jesus met the man who was lying at the pool of Bethesda waiting for a miracle, He asked him how long he had been lying there crippled. I think He asked that question just to show care and compassion. He already knew that He could heal the man, but was interested enough to want to know more about him.

Do you ever find yourself not asking people questions

because you don't want to take the time to listen to their answer? I know that sounds terrible, but if we admit it, we probably all feel that way at times. We get so caught up in what we are doing that we miss opportunities to listen to and love others every day.

Words are powerful. We should all make a commitment to use our words to love people and build them up. But don't forget that we must first learn to truly listen. Every day when we leave our homes, we are going into a society that is drowning in tragedy. God has given us the ability to help others. He has given us words, and if we use them properly, they can be life changing.

CHAPTER
16

Don't Let the Devil Speak Through You

You might have been tempted to just skip over this chapter, thinking, "That certainly isn't me. I don't let the devil speak through me!" If so, I understand how you might feel, but please read on just in case there is something here for you to learn.

If we allow the devil to speak through us, then we are in a manner of speaking "working for him." For example, he is referred to as "the Accuser of the brethren." That means he continually brings accusation against the children of God, trying to accuse them to God, to make them feel guilty and condemned, and even to cause others to think accusing thoughts about them. If we allow that accusing spirit to work through us, then we will easily and quickly find fault with many people and things. The devil also accuses us to ourselves. He places accusing thoughts in our minds, or brings accusation from other people. The Bible says that we overcome him by the blood of the Lamb, and the word of our testimony (see Revelation 12:10–11). If we know the truth of God's Word and act on it, we can defeat the devil!

The devil magnifies faults—ours and other people's. Unless we truly listen to God, we will focus only on faults and fail to see the good in ourselves or other people. Satan and anyone influenced by him always focuses on what is wrong and they blow it out of proportion so that it seems even bigger and worse than what it truly is.

Cast Out the Faultfinder

The devil is a faultfinder, and if we only focus on what is wrong in life and with ourselves and other people, then we are taking our nature from him. However, God has given us a new nature if we are truly His children and we must learn to function from the renewed part of our being. The Bible says we are to put off the old man and put on the new man that is re-created in Jesus Christ (see Ephesians 4:22–24). *Put on* and *put off* are phrases that require us to take action that often goes beyond how we feel. If we are going to operate in the new nature God has given us, then we will have to initially begin by doing it on purpose. As we follow the leading of our renewed spirit and the Holy Spirit Who dwells in us, we will develop new habits, but it does take time. God operates on the principle of "gradual growth," and that means things change little by little. To see the fullness of God's plan come to pass, we must be patient and learn to celebrate our progress. We need to recognize how far we have come in reaching our goals, and not only see how far we still have to go.

I will admit that for many years of my life I was definitely a faultfinder, and in being that way, I was helping the enemy in his cause, but I didn't know that I was. Even though I was a Christian, I was letting the devil use my mouth. I was ignorant of many of the principles of God, and especially how important my words were. I not only noticed people's faults, but told them and other people all about them. I was a faultfinder, a gossiper, a slanderer, and an accuser, and I am not proud of it, but I did have to admit it in order to find freedom from it. I want to encourage you to be honest with yourself even though it is usually very painful for us to do so. Are you one who easily notices what is wrong with everything and everyone? Or are you more inclined to see the good in life and people? If you do notice what is wrong, are you able to reason with yourself and say, "I have faults also, and God has not called me to judge and condemn, but to pray for and love people"? Or do you not only see what is wrong, but talk about it to whoever will listen?

Not only do we tend to talk about what is wrong with people, but we also lean toward talking about what is wrong in the world, the government, our jobs, neighborhoods, et cetera. I can honestly say that most of what I hear people talking about is something that is wrong somewhere or with somebody. It is true that we have a lot of evil in the world today, but God is still working and He is greater than anything or anyone. Let's talk about all the good we can and recount and recall all of the wonderful things that God has made, has done, and is doing. Let us magnify God rather than the works of wickedness that we see around us.

Negative talk is very unattractive to God, and actually, He

hates it. Thankfully He does love us unconditionally, but it really saddens Him when we use the power of words in such a negative way. He knows the damage they do and wants us to know it also.

In speaking of unbelievers, the apostle Paul says "they were filled...with every kind of unrighteousness, iniquity, grasping and covetous greed, and malice. [They were] full of envy and jealousy, murder, strife, deceit and treachery, ill will, and cruel ways. [They were] secret backbiters and gossipers" (Romans 1:29). If these are the traits of unbelievers, then those of us who consider ourselves believers in God and His children certainly shouldn't display these traits. I also find it interesting that Paul places gossip in the same list as murder and deceit. I think this should wake us up and help us realize how serious these sins are.

Women Beware

If you wouldn't write it and sign it, don't say it.
—Earl Wilson

A few times the Bible singles out women, telling them not to gossip.

[The] women likewise must be worthy of respect and serious, not gossipers, but temperate and self-controlled, [thoroughly] trustworthy in all things.
1 Timothy 3:11

Women must not only avoid gossiping, but also be trust-worthy. And that means we must keep people's secrets. Of course, the same thing applies to men, but this scripture singles out women. Women are more likely to fall prey to these types of "word sins" than men. I honestly cannot imagine Dave going out for a day of golf and he and his buddies talking about some of the things that I hear women talk about. As far as keeping secrets goes, Dave is much better at it than I am. For example, if we plan to do something really cool for our children for Christmas, I cannot wait to tell them, but Dave would say, "Just wait till Christmas," and it wouldn't matter to him if Christmas were eleven months away.

Proverbs tells us about the virtuous woman, and it says:

She looks well to how things go in her household, and the bread of idleness (gossip, discontent and self-pity) she will not eat.   *Proverbs 31:27*

The apostle Paul sent instructions to Timothy on how to handle widows and who true widows are. He said that younger widows should not be put on the rolls as someone the church would provide for; otherwise they might get bored and wander from house to house as idlers and busy-bodies, saying what they should not say and talking of things that they should not mention (see 1 Timothy 5:11–13). I find it to be interesting that Paul teaches to keep younger women busy working or raising families so they don't get bored and start gossiping. Older women have hopefully gained wisdom and know how to use their time wisely in doing good deeds for others, but young or old, the trait of gossip is definitely a symptom of spiritual immaturity.

What About Men?

The apostle Paul also writes specifically to men stating that a leader should not be a new convert, lest his mind be clouded by pride and he fall into a stupid state of mind thinking more highly of himself than he ought. Paul also mentioned that the new convert might get involved in slander and fall into the devil's trap (see 1 Timothy 3:6–7). We see that gossip and slander are the devil's business, and when we allow him to use our mouth for it, we have fallen into his trap. We also see that this type of behavior is not suitable for anyone in a position of leadership of any type.

Men or women who talk too much must beware of gossiping, spreading rumors, and not keeping people's secrets. A gossiper is a very dangerous person. It seems we all like to tell a tale and we usually add a bit to it. By the time it goes through a dozen people, it may become a wicked, ungodly tale that is used to destroy people's reputations and lives.

I recently read an item that I want to share with you. It is called, "I Am Gossip," and it's a powerful reminder of the qualities of gossip.

I Am Gossip

My name is gossip.

I have no respect for justice.

I maim without killing. I break hearts and ruin lives.

I am cunning, malicious and gather strength with age.

The more I am quoted, the more I am believed.

I flourish at every level of society.

My victims are helpless.

They cannot protect themselves against me because I have no name and no face.

To track me down is impossible. The harder you try, the more elusive I become.

I am nobody's friend.

Once I tarnish a reputation, it is never the same.

I topple governments and wreck marriages. I ruin careers and cause sleepless nights, heartaches and indigestion.

I spawn suspicion and generate grief.

I make innocent people cry in their pillows. Even my name hisses.

I am called GOSSIP, office gossip—shop gossip—party gossip—telephone gossip. I make headlines and headaches. REMEMBER, when you repeat a story, ask yourself: Is it true? Is it fair? Is it necessary? If not, do not repeat it. KEEP QUIET!

Sometimes the power of no words is the greatest power of all! Sir Winston Churchill said, "By swallowing evil words unsaid, no one has ever harmed his stomach."

We all need to be strong in resisting the devil's temptations to say things that are hurtful and needless. He loves to use us for his dirty work, but God wants to use us for His glory. God wants to use our words to encourage, but the devil wants to use them to discourage, destroy reputations, or break another's spirit. Many people are left brokenhearted because of unkind, untrue words spoken to them or about them.

A special word of caution to parents: We must be careful as parents not to be too hard on our children or we might break their spirit. That means the child would merely give up and find no courage to try to do what is right. If we find too much fault with people and don't ever give encouragement, they soon become overwhelmed and feel as if they can't please us no matter what they do. Don't gossip about your children's faults to anyone, and if at all possible, correct them in private in order to prevent others from forming a critical opinion of them. If you have adult children, don't repeat to another of your children what one has done to displease you. Gossip within the family stirs up strife, but love *covers* a multitude of sins.

Anytime I need to correct an employee, I always tell the person what he is doing and has done right before telling him what he's doing wrong. Some liquid medicines contain sugar, otherwise they would be almost impossible to swallow. People can receive or swallow our corrections much better if they are coated in a little sugar. Do the same things with your children when you need to correct them. Don't tell them what they are doing wrong without telling them what they do right!

Correction is necessary. God corrects and chastises those whom He loves, but He also compliments, blesses, rewards, and honors them. Be sure you make a big deal out of everything your children or anyone else under your authority does well, and they will love and trust you enough to receive godly correction from you.

The Slanderer

If the serpent bites before it is charmed, then it is no use to call a charmer [and the slanderer is no better than the uncharmed snake].   *Ecclesiastes 10:11*

Wow! That is a strong scripture, and it makes me realize how serious it is to slander another person. According to *Vine's Dictionary of the Bible*, the word *slanderer* is *diabolos* in the Greek language. This same Greek word is one of the names given to the devil, and means "an accuser, a slanderer, or to malign." A slanderer is someone who is given to finding fault with the demeanor and conduct of others, and spreading innuendos and criticisms.

When we say slanderous things about people to others, we literally poison their spirit and attitude toward them. The Bible says that we make them a victim.

The words of a whisperer or slanderer are like dainty morsels or words of sport [to some, but to others are like deadly wounds]; and they go down into the innermost parts of the body [or of the victim's nature].   *Proverbs 26:22*

Careful examination of this scripture teaches us a lot. First of all, what is sport or amusement to one person can be a deadly wound to another. We may enjoy giving our negative opinions about people, but they go down into the "victim's" innermost parts. The person we are talking to either believes the report, or even if he chooses not to believe it, he still has to resist the suspicion that continues to rise up in his mind.

A few days ago I saw someone that I knew at a gathering, and a few seconds after I asked how he was, he told me something he had heard that was very critical about someone we both knew. It was a rumor, and the person telling me had no proof and no reason to tell me the story. I listened for a minute and then I said, "I will not believe that unless I know it for a fact." However, I have still had the slander come back to my thoughts a few times and found myself wondering, "Can that possibly be true?" The person I was talking to has been a Christian for a long time and probably knew it was wrong to relay the story, but he did it anyway. Gossip is a type of verbal terrorism.

> To destroy somebody's good name is to commit a kind of murder.   *Rabbi Joseph Telushkin*

How often do we say something to someone and walk off thinking no more about it, but we have poisoned their innermost being with our venomous words? Slander is a serious problem, and it is time that we all stop letting the devil use our mouths for it. This is definitely an area where we should apply what is commonly called the Golden Rule: "Do unto others as you would have them do unto you." If we all stopped and asked ourselves, "Would I want someone to say this about me?" before slandering another, we'd probably refrain from speaking ill of others.

Why did the person I was talking to say what he did even though I suspect he knew it was wrong? It is because what the apostle James said is absolutely true: "And the tongue is a fire. [The tongue is a] world of wickedness set among our members, contaminating and depraving the whole body and setting on fire the wheel of birth (the cycle of man's nature), being itself ignited by hell" (James 3:6).

We must remember that using our words in a way that tears others down is one of the strongest temptations we face, and we cannot tame our tongues without trusting God to convict us of sin anytime we start to say something that is not pleasing to Him. God will do His part, but then we must be committed to respond with obedience. I was talking on the phone to a friend this morning and was asked about a troubling situation we have been dealing with. We talked for a few minutes and I started feeling upset emotionally, so I just said to her, "It is best if I don't talk about this, because all it does is upset me." I handled it properly this time, but many times in the past I would have kept talking even though I was getting a loving reminder from the Holy Spirit to stop.

Jesus said that we should stop allowing ourselves to be upset and disturbed, and instead we should enjoy the peace that He left us (see John 14:27). Since peace is His will and the Bible firmly teaches us to follow peace and let it be the umpire in our lives, deciding with finality all things that need decisions, it wasn't that difficult for me to realize that if I was feeling upset, I needed to stop talking. Why continue talking until I was so upset that I might have spent the rest of the day miserable?

What we were discussing wasn't a slanderous situation, but it was causing me to lose my peace and I knew I needed to stop talking. I have also experienced times when I was talking about someone and started losing my peace and knew that I needed to stop. One of the main ways that God speaks to us is through His peace. If we have it, then we have a green light and can proceed forward with our current actions. But if we have lost that wonderful peace, it is a red light and means STOP.

Slander, gossip, backbiting, and faultfinding are sins, and they should not be looked at as "acceptable" sins, as they often are. These types of words and conversations are not acceptable to God, and they spiritually damage us, and those we talk to.

How to Handle a Slanderer

It is important for us to know how to handle someone in our presence that is slandering another. What should you do if you are with a friend who begins gossiping about someone? Believe it or not, the advice may be different depending on whether you are with a believer or an unbeliever.

If you are with an unbeliever who has no knowledge that their behavior is wrong, you might have to just wait until you can find a good way to get away from the conversation without being too obvious. Make sure that you don't participate in any slander or agree with it, but correcting the person might alienate her and probably close the door to any future opportunity you might have to share your faith in God with her. Another thing we can do in a situation like this is to gently try to turn the conversation to a more positive one by inserting some good comments about the one being slandered.

If you are with a Christian who does know better, then to sit idly by and say or do nothing is wrong. You might say something like, "I really don't want to talk about this," or "I don't think it is right for us to talk about this," or "There are two sides to every story and we don't know enough to form an opinion." Paul taught that we should correct those over-taken in sin or misconduct courteously, keeping an attentive eye on ourselves lest we also fall into sin (see Galatians 6:1). All too often we sit by and do nothing, using the excuse that we don't want to hurt anyone's feelings. When we do this, we are not helping others or ourselves. You wouldn't sit by while a friend robbed a bank, would you? Of course you wouldn't do that, so then why do you sit by while a friend slanders or gossips? It is only because these sins have become acceptable in society, but that does not make them right.

The Bible teaches us that in the last days, evil will increase. It says that people will be lovers of self and utterly self-centered. They will be proud, boasters, disrespectful, unholy, slanderers (false accusers), and troublemakers, loose in morals, haters of what is good, et cetera (see 2 Timothy 3:3).

We are in the world and cannot always avoid all the people who engage in behavior as we have mentioned, but we must avoid joining in with them. In order to be a good example to unbelievers or even believers who are sinning, we must be careful not to do what they do. We don't want to give the impression that we think we are better than they are, but we must lovingly, humbly, and gently decline to be involved in conversation and other behaviors that we know are displeasing to God.

The apostle Paul told the Corinthians not to associate

with a believer who was "guilty of immorality or greed" or "an idolater" or "a person with a foul tongue [railing, abusing, reviling, slandering]" (1 Corinthians 5:11). It seems to me after studying this verse of scripture that I could more easily associate (not closely) with an unbeliever doing these things than someone who bears the name of Christian.

I believe we are obligated in love to gently remind other Christians that they should not slander, and we ought to pray for friends who will also hold us accountable in areas of our own conduct. It is embarrassing to have someone say, "You shouldn't be talking like that"; however, it usually puts an end to it, and hopefully teaches a lesson.

In this same chapter, Paul told the Corinthians not to associate closely and habitually with impure people. He said, however, that we could not avoid them altogether; otherwise we would have to get out of the world. But then he said not to associate or even eat a meal with someone claiming to be a Christian who indulges in these immoral behaviors.

In bringing up these verses, I am probably opening a can of worms, and I can almost hear your questions right now. For example, "Joyce, I am married to an unbeliever and he gossips all the time about everyone. Are you telling me not to associate with him?" I think the answer to this question is to use wisdom. You cannot avoid the people in your own immediate family, but you don't have to choose to have a slanderer for a good friend. You don't have to sit at a lunch table each day where all the people are slandering the boss. When a Christian friend slanders someone, you should tell her that you don't want to hear it, or that you will not believe it without proof. We would not eat poison if it was offered to us, so why should we be involved in something that God specifically tells us will poison our innermost parts?

Let us choose to speak words of life and not death. Not one of us should be guilty of letting the devil use our mouth to harm or destroy the reputation of another. If after reading this chapter you realize that perhaps you have been working for the devil by lending him your mouth, then turn in your resignation today and never go back to work for him again.

old wax

CHAPTER
17

Do You Really Have to Give Your Opinion?

In the previous chapter we uncovered a problem that we all deal with in some way or another. We are either guilty of gossip, faultfinding, slander, and backbiting, or we deal with people who are. We know that the devil is the root cause of all these sins, but our desire to give our opinion is also involved. Why is it so important for us to tell people what we think?

Giving one's opinion when nobody is asking for it is a major source of relationship problems, and also the cause of a lot of the "word sins" we have been discussing.

We have opinions about what people should wear, who they should and shouldn't marry, what kind of home they buy, the car they drive, their hairstyle, and even how they invest their money. In our pride, we tend to think that everyone should do what we are doing or would do, and when they don't, it leads to us judging them, being critical, gossiping, and possibly slandering them. Just think about it—all these huge problems came from an inordinate desire to give our opinion.

Mind Your Own Business

Make it your ambition and definitely endeavor to live quietly and peacefully, to mind your own affairs, and to work with your hands, as we charged you.   *1 Thessalonians 4:11*

A sincere consideration of this scripture reveals several things. First, living peacefully must be our ambition, and we will have to work at it. When the writer of Thessalonians says we must *"definitely endeavor"* to live quietly and peacefully, he is saying it will need to be a goal we pursue zealously. We must also be willing to make whatever changes necessary in order to reach this goal. Second, if we wish to reach the goal of peace, we will need to learn to mind our own business, and instead give ourselves to the work we are called to do. If you are a person who freely gives out opinions, but you are ready to change, then the first step toward change is to admit it is a problem in your life and ask God to help you change.

My entire family is opinionated, including me, so I know firsthand the challenge of minding my own business. With God's help and lots of contemplation, I have made a lot of progress, but I still have to discipline myself to keep quiet about my own opinions when I am tempted to get involved in a situation that is truly none of my business. We all have enough business of our own to tend to, without needing to get involved in other people's uninvited. God's Word tells us to "discover not and disclose not another's secret" (Proverbs 25:9). We are curious and often quite nosy and are tempted to get into other people's business. We just plain like to know, or think we know, what is going on everywhere, and it ends up stealing our peace. Did you ever dig around and find out something, and then wished you had not? I certainly know that I have. Although God wants us to be knowledgeable, it is the right kind of knowledge that He wants us to have. When it comes to discovering the secrets of others, we can apply the saying "What we don't know can't hurt us." I have come to realize that I can avoid a lot of drama in my life by staying out of things that are none of my business. Plato said, "Wise men talk because they have something to say; fools talk because they have to say something."

I like to know the "why" of things, so let's ponder why we are so opinionated. I think it makes us feel superior or important to give our opinions on issues, but if we are truthful, we will also admit that doing so is the cause of many arguments. Perhaps if we come to know our value in Christ more fully, we won't search for our sense of importance in ungodly ways. A wise man or woman listens more than talks, as I have already said—God has given us two ears and one mouth as a strong indicator that we are to listen more than we talk. When we talk all the time, we rarely hear what others are saying because while they are talking, we are busy forming in our minds what we will say when they stop talking. The inordinate desire to tell others what we think and give our opinion is one sure way of recognizing insecurity in us or in others.

A secure person knows what he believes, but he has no need to tell others unless someone is truly interested. If he is asked for an opinion and finds it is met with resistance, he has no need to "convince" people that he is right.

In my younger years, I was very insecure and felt quite undone when people didn't agree with me. I found communication with my husband nearly impossible and really did not understand why. Then God revealed to me that if Dave didn't agree with me, I felt rejected, and I needed to realize he was free to have his own opinions without having to agree with me in order to make me feel good about myself. When he didn't agree, I repeatedly tried to convince him that my opinion was correct, and he ended up feeling manipulated and controlled. I recall one time saying, "We need to talk about this," and he said, "Joyce, we don't talk. You talk and want me to listen and agree with everything you say." What he said hurt, but it was true. The truth about us usually hurts, but facing it is the only pathway to freedom.

I valued my own opinion more than anyone else's, and I didn't listen with an open mind to what others had to say. The truth was that I didn't know anything at all about the things in life that truly matter because I was not a student of God's Word. I went to church, but I did not know God or His character intimately. The first sign that we are gaining wisdom is when we come to know that we don't know anything at all, and we humbly ask God to begin teaching us.

I want to add that during those years of being excessively opinionated and having deep-seated insecurity, I had no peace. My life seemed like one endless frustration! It was only after I began to crave and pursue peace that I realized that one of the causes for my lack of peace was getting involved in other people's business. Do yourself a favor and mind your own business because it will increase your peace, and an increase of peace always leads to more joy. Having peace should be more important to us than anything else, and we should be willing to do whatever we must in order to have it, including keeping our opinions to ourselves and minding our own business!

Letting Your Children Grow Up

One of the most difficult areas to mind our own business in is with our adult children. We are so accustomed to telling them what to do while they are children living at home that we must consciously make a transition into letting them live their own lives without interference from us. Dave and I have four grown children, and we spend a lot of time with them, so I have a lot of opportunity to practice minding my own business. Sometimes I am better at it than others, but thankfully I am still learning and growing all the time.

Recently one of our daughters and her husband purchased a new home, and we offered to help them with the cost of the furniture they would need. I love to play around with decorating and was excited about being involved in the project. I assumed that she would want to decorate her home like mine, or something close to that, but she chose to go totally modern. At that point my opinions began to roll out of my mouth and I quickly observed that they were not going to promote peace. After a few rounds of trying to get her to like what I liked, I reminded myself that how she decorated was really none of my business. Since we were helping financially with the project, I had to remind myself a few times to mind my own business! I had to remember that when we give, we must do it with no strings attached, or otherwise it is not a true gift, but a covert method of control. I knew these things, and teach them to others, but no matter how much we have learned, it will be tested from time to time.

She did ask for my opinion on lots of things concerning the decorating, but she also asked a few other people in the family, and it quickly became obvious that my other children could help her more than I could. Their tastes were more similar to hers, and it just made everything easier for me to enjoy paying the bill as a total blessing, and yet not need to give my opinion uselessly.

There were several areas that she welcomed and took my advice in, but many that she did not, and my point is that she had every right to do so. When we truly love people, we set them free to be themselves and even learn to admire what they like as a compliment to their good taste. She didn't decorate the way I would have, but she did an excellent job and her home is lovely. Everyone being different is what makes life interesting so why do we fight it so furiously? It can only be due to pride!

We have grown a lot in our family relationships and have come to an agreement that if we give an opinion and it is rejected, it is okay. We all have the right to live our own lives. We also have boundaries, and that is very important. Boundaries mean that some areas are not even open to opinions from others, and we respect one another's boundaries. Some of our children ask for advice more than others, and when they do, we give it and we are excited that they ask, but even then they don't always take our advice and we have learned not to try to "convince" them that we are right.

If you want to have healthy relationships with your adult children, you must learn to respect their right to run their own lives, and even though your sincere desire may be to "help" them, you still cannot intrude into their business. This is one of the main ways we can let our children grow up. They have to make their own choices, and sometimes that means their own mistakes. There is no better teacher than mistakes we make and have to live with for a time.

Walk in wisdom and give your opinion only when someone asks for it and then do it with humility.

Right Timing

Is there ever a time when it is right to give your opinion? The answer is "yes." Our opinions are often welcome and can truly help others, so there are times when you should give your opinion. As I have said, give your opinion with humility and don't try to convince someone else that you are right. The next acceptable time to speak up is when you sincerely know the person is headed for trouble and your only desire is to help him avoid it.

Let's say that I noticed a male employee who is married paying too much attention to another woman. I have prayed about it and believe that God wants me to speak to him. I should go in an attitude of humility, keeping an attentive eye on myself, too (see Galatians 6:1), and make him aware of how his actions appear to others, and if they continue, they will lead to trouble for all involved. I recall a time like this when the person I spoke to was very appreciative and had not realized he was being slowly brought into a situation that would have ended badly. He immediately made changes and was grateful for the advice. I have been involved in other similar cases where the people being confronted made one excuse after another, were very defensive and offended, and ended up destroying their lives.

It was my responsibility to speak to them about their behavior, but in those cases, I was not merely giving my opinion, but sharing godly wisdom.

A word spoken in due season can be one of the most valuable things in the world, but out of season, it can be very destructive.

When our opinion is merely "our opinion," it is not very valuable, but if it is based on God's wisdom, it becomes another thing entirely.

Stay Within Your Sphere of Influence

People often ask for my advice because of the position of influence God has given me. We all have a sphere of influence, an area that God has given us some authority over. I have authority over things concerning Joyce Meyer Ministries, but God has taught me that I am not the boss at home. I may be sought after for advice and asked for my opinion frequently at work, but at home I am Dave's wife, and in that sphere he has the top position of authority and should be treated with respect and admiration. I don't need to give him my opinion about his every move because it makes him feel that I don't trust him and value his ability to be the leader in our family.

Even at the office there are areas that I have responsibility for and areas that Dave has responsibility for. For example, he has always taken care of the ministry finances and makes the final decisions concerning our television and radio ministry. I am responsible for my writing, teaching, preaching, and certain areas of leadership at the office. We both know our sphere of influence and show respect for each other in theirs.

You might have a position of authority at work, but don't try to take that authority into a sphere where God has given you no authority. We should know how to assume authority when it is proper and how to accept another's authority when that is proper. If a person only knows how to boss others around, he is truly immature and very prideful.

You have authority over your children, but you have no sphere of influence over other people's children; therefore, your opinion about how they raise their children is not needed, nor is it usually welcome. We have authority over our own finances, but don't need to give our opinion regarding how other people manage theirs. People give their opinion about things others purchase, often stating that they think the person had no business buying such and such, or didn't need a new automobile, new home, or more clothes. While judging how we think others waste their money, we are often being wasteful in areas that we are blinded to by our pride.

Ask God to help you stay within your sphere of influence and don't go beyond your God-ordained borders, especially when you are uninvited.

Increase Your Peace

Each one of us can increase our peace by simply minding our own business and not giving our opinion when it is not requested. We have no ability to change other people. Only God can work within the heart of an individual and make changes that are true and lasting. The best policy is to pray when we think we see something in another person that needs to change, but we should pray with all humility, reminding God that we are aware that we have many areas in our own lives that need to change also. It is easy for us to see what is wrong with other people, but quite difficult to squarely face our own faults.

I tried to change Dave for many years and made no progress at all. He felt pressured to be what I thought he should be, and it was damaging our personal relationship. It was a great day when God broke through my stubborn pride and showed me that I had more than enough areas in my own life to work on and did not need to be working on anyone else. We can cooperate with the Holy Spirit and let Him work wonderful change in us, but as I said, we cannot change other people so why waste our time trying? It only frustrates us, steals our peace, and makes the one we are trying to change feel unloved and rejected. One sincere, heartfelt prayer can accomplish more than we could accomplish in an entire life-time by our own strength.

Every time you start to say, "I think," stop and ask yourself if you really need to say what you are about to say. I have found that if I do that, much of what I had intended to say is never spoken.

CHAPTER 18

Say Something Good or Don't Say Anything at All

It would be a wonderful world to live in if we all followed the rule of either saying something good or not saying anything at all. Just imagine how pleasant our homes, schools, jobs, church, and society in general would be. I think it would be equivalent to having the atmosphere of heaven on earth. I am certain that nobody in heaven ever speaks an unkind or bad word! Words are containers for power and they do affect the atmosphere we live in. If a home is filled with angry, bitter, critical, harsh words, the very atmosphere is heavy and oppressive. It is supercharged with strife and every evil work. If an office is filled with gossip, ungrateful attitudes, and discontent, these can be felt. People with no knowledge of God's Word may not know what it is they feel, but they dread going into the very atmosphere of the place because it depresses and discourages them. They may even be party to the problem, but they fail to realize how their words affect them and everyone around them.

This story will help make my point:

Slaves of Our Words

Once upon a time an old man spread rumors that his young neighbor was a thief. As a result, the young man was arrested. Days later the young man was proven innocent. After he was released, he sued the old man for wrongly accusing him. In court the old man told the judge: "They were just comments; they were not meant to harm anyone." The judge, before passing sentence on the case, told the old man: "Write all the things you said about him on a piece of paper. Cut them up, and on the way home, throw the pieces of paper out. Tomorrow, come back to hear the sentence."

The next day, the judge told the old man: "Before receiving the sentence, you will have to go out and gather all the pieces of paper that you threw out yesterday!"

The old man said: "I can't do that! The wind spread them and I won't know where to find them."

The judge then replied: "The same way simple comments may destroy the honor of a man to such an extent that one is not able to fix it. If you can't speak well of someone, then don't say anything."

Let's be masters of our mouths, so that we won't be slaves of our words!

There is a simple rule we can follow to guide us in our conversation: If it is good, uplifting, wholesome, and pleasant, say all you want to, but if it is evil, negative, critical, and complaining, then don't say it. Ask God to change your heart so there is not even a hint of wanting to say it. What is in our heart will eventually come out of our mouth, so we cannot change what we say unless we change what we think.

If our words agree with God, we will have what God says we can have, and we will become what He says we can be. What have you been saying? Are you reaping the harvest of your own words? Do you want to see positive change in your life and circumstances? Only a foolish person thinks he can continue doing the same thing and get a different result, so if you don't like your current harvest, change your seed. Bad seed (words) equals bad harvest, and good seed (words) equals good harvest. The more good things you speak, the more good you will experience in your life.

The word *good* means "to be desired or approved of, pleasing and welcome." The challenge of never speaking anything the rest of my life except what is good seems a bit overwhelming, but I seem to have more faith if I think of doing it one day at a time. Will you make a commitment for today not to say anything unless it is something good? When you make mistakes, don't give up, but ask for God's forgiveness and press on. Make that same commitment each and every day.

Even a fool when he holds his peace is considered wise; when he closes his lips he is esteemed a man of understanding.   *Proverbs 17:28*

Making a commitment to speak only good things does not mean that we will no longer be tempted. I can assure you that Satan will tempt you even more. He knows the power of words, and the very thought of you improving yours is frightening to him. He only has the control over us that we give him with our words. If we discipline ourselves to stop speaking evil, negative things, we close the door of opportunity that has been previously open to Satan. Satan will always tempt us to do and say what is wrong, but we can resist him. Say what God says, and you will find that no weapon formed against you can prosper.

Facing Truth

I have mentioned several times in this book the importance of facing truth because it is the only way to make progress. I don't want anyone to merely read this book and enjoy it, but I want it to have life-changing benefits. Ask God to help you make an honest evaluation of the types of words you have spoken in the past. Examining where we are will help us get to where we want to be. When I took an honest look at how I had been speaking in the past, I was not at all pleased with myself. I was sorry for the way I had wasted my words and I asked God to forgive me. I knew that God loved me unconditionally, but I also believe He grieved over the damage I was doing to my own life through speaking evil words. In searching for the source of our problems, we often find that it is right under our nose, in our mouth. You can change your life by changing your words.

The more you speak good things, the more you will dread being with people who rarely have anything good to say. Start genuinely listening to yourself and other people talk and you will quickly realize that one of the biggest problems in the world is the wrong use of words. But the good news is that we can turn things around for the good by beginning to speak only what is good.

A Happy Heart Is Good Medicine

A happy heart is good medicine, and a cheerful mind works healing, but a broken spirit dries up the bones.   *Proverbs 17:22*

Just imagine how much happier you could be in an atmosphere where only good things were spoken. No complaining, but instead thankful words spoken regularly, and no idle gossip, judgmental or critical words spoken. No negative, hopeless words, but words of hope, faith, and positive expectation. God is a huge fan of "good." He is good, all of His creation is declared to be good, He promises to do us good all the days of our lives, He works good out of every situation we commit to Him. Jesus is called the "Good Shepherd." Surely He wants us to say something good or not say anything at all.

We can immediately increase our joy by speaking right words. The more I ponder it, the more amazed I am that I can immediately increase or decrease my joy and the joy of others by simply choosing to say good things. Do yourself a favor and say something good!

Joy is vital! Nehemiah tells us that our joy is our strength. No wonder the devil works overtime trying to do anything he can to diminish our joy and make us sad, depressed, discouraged, and filled with despair. Don't sit by and let it happen to you. Fight the good fight of faith with faith-filled words that will release joy into the very atmosphere you are in.

The Gospel message is referred to in the Bible as the Good News! Jesus came to bring Good News and glad tidings of great joy. There is nothing sad about Jesus. He came to destroy the works of the wicked one, to overcome evil with good. If Jesus had come to earth and talked only about His circumstances and how bad they were, and all the wicked people and how bad they were, how bad the government was, et cetera, we would still be hopeless and lost in our sin. But Jesus came preaching the Good News, the goodness of God, and the fruit of goodness. He wants us to be as committed to finding and magnifying the good in everything as He was.

Anything Good Makes Me Happy

God is the author of all good, and the very thought of anything "good" increases my joy. I love to do good things for people, and I enjoy it when people do good things for me. I love to hear good reports and testimonies, and I love it when people tell me something good they have heard someone else say about me. I am sure that makes you happy, too. On the other hand, think how it makes you feel if you hear that someone has said something bad about you. Bad things make us feel bad, and good things make us feel good, so why not be committed to doing and saying all the good you can?

I love good smells, anything that is good and beautiful to look at, and I love the Good Shepherd! I love the Good News of the Gospel! I love good weather, good days, good parties, good movies, and good-looking clothes! I think I may as well admit that I am simply addicted to good!

> See that none of you repays another with evil for evil, but always *aim* to show kindness and *seek* to do good to one another and to everybody.   *1 Thessalonians 5:15 (emphasis mine)*

I want to emphasize the words *aim* and *seek*, to call attention to the fact that doing good is possible only when we actively seek to do so. Make doing good, being good, and speaking good things your goals in life. If you do, then you can expect more joy than you have ever experienced.

God Is Good

I doubt that I have to convince you that God is good, but just in case you ever wonder, look at just a sample of what the Bible says about Him.

> O taste and see that the Lord [our God] is good! Blessed (happy, fortunate, to be envied) is the man who trusts and takes refuge in Him.   *Psalm 34:8*
>
> For You, O Lord, are good, and ready to forgive [our trespasses, sending them away, letting them go completely and forever].   *Psalm 86:5*

O give thanks to the Lord, for He is good; for His mercy and loving-kindness endure forever.   *Psalm 136:1*
How great is God's goodness, and how great is His beauty.   *Zechariah 9:17*

If you feel that you have not experienced the goodness of God, don't blame Him. Ask yourself if your words have been strong and hard against Him. In the Book of Malachi, God told the people to tithe and bring offerings of all their increase and that He would open the windows of heaven and pour out blessings so great they could not contain them. However, not only did the people not choose to do what God instructed them to do in their giving, but their words were strong and hard against Him. This is what they said:

Your words have been strong and hard against Me, says the Lord. Yet you say, What have we spoken against You?
You have said, It is useless to serve God, and what profit is it if we keep His ordinances and walk gloomily and as if in mourning apparel before the Lord of hosts?   *Malachi 3:13–14*

These people had not obeyed God and then they foolishly blamed Him for the result they got. They said it is no use to serve God. Some people still say those kinds of things when they don't get an immediate result from their obedience. Faith and patience must work together. While you are waiting for your circumstances to improve, the words that you speak are vitally important. Don't let your words be strong and hard against God. Even when you see no evidence of it, keep saying, "God is good, He has a good plan for my life, and something good is going to happen to me today!"

If you have been convicted that you definitely need to change what you say, you must expect that it will take time for the good words to produce a good harvest. Don't do what is right merely to get a right result. Do right because it is right, and God will take care of your harvest at exactly the right time.

Just remember that the "Good Book" introduces us to the "Good Shepherd," Who brings "Good News," and introduces us to the "Good Life" He preordained for us to live. He wants us to say good things and be good to everyone! This simple, yet profound principle can and will change the world.

If you can't say something good, then don't say anything at all.

CHAPTER
19

Gentle Words

*Constant kindness can accomplish much. As the sun
makes ice melt, kindness causes misunderstanding,
mistrust, and hostility to evaporate.*
—Albert Schweitzer

Gentleness is also kindness, meekness, and humility, and it is a display of love. The Holy Spirit manifested in the form of a dove, which is a very gentle bird. The Holy Spirit is like our tender mother, always gentle and kind even in the midst of chastisement and correction.

Humility is said to be the chief virtue and more than likely the most difficult to grow into. A humble person is totally dependent on God for all things, and she never thinks more highly of herself than she ought to. She doesn't consider that she is superior to any other person. When a person has a humble heart and attitude, it always shows through in how she speaks to and about other people. It is also evident in how she talks about her own lot in life.

Humility never has an attitude of entitlement, and it considers every tiny blessing to be undeserved and a gift from

God. Therefore, it doesn't complain and murmur about its life. It waits patiently for God to change whatever circumstances He desires, and trusts that He will give the needed strength to endure whatever must be endured with good temper.

God's Word states the virtuous woman has "the law of kindness" on her tongue (Proverbs 31:26). She speaks kindly to everyone, and that happens only when one is meek and humble, seeing everyone as equally important. I will admit that for many years I did not have a humble attitude and neither was I gentle in the way I spoke to and about others. Pride can be heard in our words, and even our voice tones. Pride has a sound of criticism in much of what it says. It is demeaning and belittling. True love is kind, and it understands the power of kindness. Mother Teresa said, "Kind words can be short and easy to speak but their echoes are endless." When we speak words of kindness or do acts of kindness, they always return to bless us. "The merciful, kind, and generous man benefits himself [for his deeds return to bless him]," says Proverbs 11:17.

Words of affirmation are among the kindest words you can ever utter. John Trent tells the following story of Mary, a little girl who was different from everyone else.

Mary had grown up knowing that she was different from the other kids, and she hated it. She was born with a cleft palate and had to bear the jokes and stares of cruel children who teased her nonstop about her misshaped lip, crooked nose, and garbled speech. With all the teasing, Mary grew up hating the fact that she was "different." She was convinced that no one outside her family could ever love her—until she entered Mrs. Leonard's class.

Mrs. Leonard had a warm smile, a round face, and shiny brown hair. While everyone in her class liked her, Mary came to love Mrs. Leonard. In the 1950s, it was common for teachers to give their children an annual hearing test. However, in Mary's case, in addition to her cleft palate, she was barely able to hear out of one ear. Determined not to let the other children have another "difference" to point out, she would cheat on the test each year. The "whisper test" was given by having a child walk to the classroom door, turn sideways, close one ear with a finger, and then repeat something that the teacher whispered. Mary turned her bad ear toward her teacher and pretended to cover her good ear. She knew that teachers would often say things like, "The sky is blue," or "What color are your shoes?" But not on that day. Surely God put seven words in Mrs. Leonard's mouth that changed Mary's life forever. When the "whisper test" came, Mary heard these words: "I wish you were my little girl."

If someone were to pay you 10 cents for every kind word you have ever spoken and collect 5 cents from you for every unkind word, would you be rich or poor?

Kindness pays:

One day, Howard Kelly, a poor boy who was selling goods from door to door to pay his way through school, found he had only one thin dime left, and he was hungry.

He decided he would ask for a meal at the next house. However, he lost his nerve when a lovely young woman opened the door. Instead of a meal he asked for a drink of water. She thought he looked hungry so brought him a large glass of milk. He drank it slowly, and then asked, "How much do I owe you?"

"You don't owe me anything," she replied. "Mother has taught us never to accept payment for a kindness." He said, "Then I thank you from my heart."

As Howard left that house, not only did he feel stronger physically, but his faith in God and man was strong also. He had been ready to give up and quit.

Years later that young woman became critically ill. The local doctors were baffled. They finally sent her to the big city, where they called in specialists to study her rare disease. Dr. Howard Kelly was called in for the consultation. When he heard the name of the town she came from, a strange light filled his eyes.

Immediately he rose and went down the hall of the hospital to her room. He recognized her at once. He went back to the consultation room determined to do his best to save her life. From that day on, he gave special attention to the case.

After a long struggle, the battle was won. Dr. Kelly requested the business office to pass the final bill to him for approval. He looked at it, then wrote something on the edge, and the bill was sent to her room. She was afraid to open it, for she was sure it would take the rest of her life to pay for it all. Finally she looked, and something caught her attention on the side as she read these words: "Paid in full with one glass of milk." Signed: Dr. Howard Kelly.

Her kind words, "You don't owe me anything," to a young man in need came back to her many years later in the same manner. A few kind words and a random act of kindness changed a young man's life, and they returned to save her life years later and she didn't owe anything!

Pride Is Always Jealous and Speaks Harshly

David had been anointed by the prophet Samuel to be the future king of Israel, and his brothers were jealous. Pride is always jealous, because it assumes that it deserves what others have. When the giant Goliath was mocking the army of Israel and none of the soldiers took any action against him, David came to see the battle for himself. He was amazed that everyone stood idly by while this uncircumcised Philistine jeered at and mocked the armies of the living God. He asked what might be done for the man who defeated the giant, and his brother Eliab was enraged.

> Now Eliab his eldest brother heard what he said to the men; and Eliab's anger was kindled against David and he said, Why did you come here? With whom have you left those few sheep in the wilderness? I know your presumption and evilness of heart; for you came down that you might see the battle.   *1 Samuel 17:28*

The very sight of David angered Eliab, and we can clearly hear his pride in all that he says to David. Notice that he tried to belittle David by reminding him that all he did was care for a few sheep in the wilderness, and who did he think he was to come among the "important soldiers" and begin to question them? Then Eliab accused David of the very sins that were in his own heart (presumption and evilness). Pride often accuses another of what it is guilty of, but has failed to see. Prideful people are so busy judging and being critical of others that they are blinded to their own misconduct by their pride.

My father was a harsh, hard-hearted, and mean man. He always belittled others and rarely said a kind word about anyone. He was never gentle. Because I was always treated and talked to harshly, I became harsh in my own speech and mannerisms. I found this trait quite difficult to overcome, but I did seek ardently to change it.

Let Jesus Be Your Example

Take My yoke upon you and learn of Me, for I am gentle (meek) and humble (lowly) in heart.

For My yoke is wholesome (useful, good—not harsh, hard, sharp, or pressing, but comfortable, gracious, and pleasant).   *Matthew 11:29–30*

Jesus invites us to stay close to Him and learn how He handles every situation in life. He is gentle, meek, and humble, not harsh, hard, sharp, or pressing. He is comfortable to be in relationship with. Are you? Can people be at ease around you, or do they feel tense because they know if they do anything that displeases you even slightly, they will have to endure harsh words of criticism? There was a time in my life when I created that kind of "on edge" atmosphere in my own home. I had been treated harshly, and the very treatment that I despised was the way I treated others. I am so glad that

God is gentle, forgiving, kind, and merciful. His gentleness has healed me and is available to us all.

It's All in Your Mind

Facing pride and developing humility are two of the most important things in our life because they affect everything we do and say. In order for our words to be gentle, we need to have a humble heart and attitude, and that comes only from having a humble mind. We can purposely think things that will help us behave in a manner that is pleasing to God. I call them "think sessions." Take time to think like this: "I am not superior to anyone else. All of my abilities are gifts from God, and not anything that I have is apart from Him. We are all equal in God's eyes, and I choose to treat every person I meet with the utmost respect. When I speak to people, I do so with the utmost humility and display meekness and gentleness at all times. The Law of Kindness is on my tongue."

For by the grace (unmerited favor of God) given to me I warn everyone among you not to estimate and think of himself more highly than he ought [not to have an exaggerated opinion of his own importance], but to rate his ability with sober judgment, each according to the degree of faith apportioned by God to him.   *Romans 12:3*

Have a meeting with yourself daily, and the earlier in the day, the better it will be. Have a chat with yourself, reminding yourself that you are not better than anyone else, not always right, and that you have no authority to judge and be critical of other people. God alone is judge of all things. Plan ahead of time to be gentle with everyone you meet and even more so when it is a wounded individual who desperately needs kindness and understanding.

Learn to recognize pride in yourself. If you listen carefully, you will hear it come out in your words when it is in your heart. Do not permit it to remain, but purposely put on humility and do what you believe Jesus would do in every situation.

The Bible says that we are to clothe ourselves with humility (see 1 Peter 5:5), and I believe this is something we should do purposefully. I never put my clothes on in the morning without thinking over what I want to wear and how it will look on me. Then I purposely put it on. Clothing ourselves with humility works the same way. Think it over and ask: What kind of attitude will look good on you? What spiritual virtues would God like to see you wear today? Will He be pleased if we are clothed with pride, haughtiness, harshness, and hardness? We know that He would not, so we must make the effort with His help to develop the virtue of humility so that our words will be gentle and kind.

Be Firm and Direct

When I speak of being gentle and kind, that doesn't negate the need for occasional firmness when we deal with certain individuals. There are times when we need to be firm with our children and let them see our displeasure with their behavior. Jesus was certainly straightforward and firm when He spoke to the Pharisees and religious leaders of His day about their critical and unloving attitudes. He called them a brood of vipers, whitewashed tombs filled with dead men's bones (see Matthew 3:7, 23:27). We can hardly think that He did so with a sweet, soft voice, but His heart's motive in correcting them was still kind and gentle because His desire was to help them.

Love sometimes must be tough in its choices and decisions about how to deal with people. For example, it is often harder to say "no" to your children, whom you love, than it would be to say "yes." Yet you know that you must say "no" for their own good. If they persist in their request, you will have to be firm in your decision, and this usually means firm voice tones. However, being firm doesn't mean yelling in anger, making accusations, and recalling verbally everything they have ever done wrong. Be direct; stay calm, firm, and decisive, but try not to let your emotions rule. When we behave emotionally, we often lose the respect of the person we are attempting to deal with.

I tell you this from experience because I did it all wrong, especially with my oldest son, and when he became an adult, he told me how my words made him feel and it wasn't anything I was proud of. I yelled and threatened outrageous punishment, such as "You're not going out of this house for three months," and then I didn't follow through. I became emotional and spoke out of those emotions rather than from wisdom. Dave, on the other hand, stayed calm and firm. He explained what our son had done wrong, often told him what the Word of God said about his behavior, and then told him what would happen if he didn't change. Whatever punishment Dave did dole out was a promise, and our son knew it. With me, he knew most of what I said would change when I calmed down so he paid no attention at all to me.

Minister Life to Others

A gentle tongue [with its healing power] is a tree of life, but willful contrariness in it breaks down the spirit.   *Proverbs 15:4*

I think we should all ask ourselves how people feel after they leave our presence. Do they sense life or death? The power of both are in the tongue, and a gentle tongue is a tree of life. Gentleness can be displayed in both words and tones of voice. We might say the right words yet do so with a tone of voice that betrays our true feelings. As I began desiring to be a gentle person who walked in humility and meekness, I really tried to say the correct thing, but I still often felt that I had offended people. God had to teach me that although my words had improved, my heart attitude had not, and it was revealed in my tone of voice. I might say to Dave, "Will you please turn the lights off when you leave a room!" There is nothing wrong with the words, but if I am being sarcastic or critical, it will still come through in my tone of voice and even my body language.

I would like to say that I was just naturally a gentle soul, but I wasn't, and I had to do a lot of praying and soul searching while making progress in this area. Some of you may be naturally sweet and gentle, and if so, you may not know how blessed you are. You perhaps have more difficulty being firm and confronting issues when you need to. But if you are more like I was and tend to be harsh in your dealing with people, I urge you to immediately begin praying, studying, and working with the Holy Spirit to have a gentle tongue that is a tree of life.

When you ask people in your immediate family to do something, try not to sound as if you are giving an order. Be kind in how you ask, and you're more likely to get a favorable response. At one time, a simple request from me to take the trash out sounded like an order given by an army sergeant. I have learned that is not the way Jesus makes requests, and we can follow His example with His help, if we truly want to.

I want everyone I meet to feel better than they did before I met them. I want to minister life and I know that one of the major ways I do so is with my words. Use words carefully because they are one of the most powerful things that God has given you. And be careful about voice tones, because they reveal your heart.

CHAPTER 20

Keeping Your Word

One of the "mouth sins" that God convicted me of was telling people I would do something and then not doing it. When we lack integrity, we find it easy to talk, but if we don't feel like following through, then we just don't. God always keeps His Word, and He expects us to keep ours. That means we need to be very careful about what we tell people we will do. Yes, this is another area in which we need to be careful what we say.

Count the cost of everything before you verbally commit to do it. Think about what it will take, how long it will take, what you already have going on in your life, and if adding another thing will stress you out.

She considers a [new] field before she buys or accepts it [expanding prudently and not courting neglect of her present duties by assuming other duties]. *Proverbs 31:16*

The wise woman not only wants to avoid stress, but also wants to maintain her integrity, so she seriously thinks about things before saying she will do them. We would save ourselves a great deal of trouble in life if we would do this.

One of the greatest problems we encounter today is dealing with people who don't do what they say they will do. When we built our home, it was totally ridiculous how often we would have an appointment with a repairman or contractor and then he didn't show up or even call to say he was not coming. We had worked our schedule around that appointment and made sure we were home for it. But he totally ignored his commitment.

It is bad enough for anyone to behave this way, but when a Christian does it, to me it is doubly bad. I was recently asked what I found to be the most challenging thing in networking with other people in accomplishing greater goals. I quickly said, "Too many people simply don't do what they say they will do." I don't have time for that kind of behavior at this point in my life, and I only want to work with people who have integrity and are committed to doing what they say they will do. There will be times when we find we cannot fulfill an obligation, but at the very least we need to contact the person and say one of two things: *I should never have told you I would do that. I spoke emotionally and now find I cannot follow through.* Or explain what has happened to prevent you from keeping your word at this time and ask to be released from the commitment.

A Guilty Conscience

It is my opinion that anytime we don't keep our word, it weighs heavily on our conscience. We may have gotten good at ignoring it, or perhaps there are many things that make us feel guilty and we are unable to distinguish exactly what is the source of the feeling. But a guilty conscience prevents us from having confidence before God. King David was a man who seemed to have great confidence in his relationship with God and he often spoke of his integrity. Consider these two scriptures:

> O keep me, Lord, and deliver me; let me not be ashamed or disappointed for my trust and my refuge are in You.
> Let integrity and uprightness preserve me, for I wait for and expect You.   *Psalm 25:20–21*
> Vindicate me, O Lord, for I have walked in my integrity; I have [expectantly] trusted in, leaned on, and relied on the Lord without wavering and I shall not slide.   *Psalm 26:1*

You will notice that David boldly expected God to deliver him from his enemies, mentioning that he walked in integrity and uprightness. We know that we don't earn God's help through our own righteousness, and that He often helps those who don't deserve it. But David was a man who knew God's Word and was expected to live by it. I find it interesting that he mentioned his integrity to God as a reason why he should be preserved and delivered. He expected God's vindication. He could not have done so if he'd had a guilty conscience.

When we sin, we can admit it and ask God for forgiveness, but when we do things that are wrong and either make excuses for them or ignore them entirely, they do weigh heavily on our conscience.

It is important for each of us to do the very best that we can in every area of life. God expects us to strive for excellence because He is excellent. Part of being an excellent person is always doing what you tell people you will do. Even a statement such as "I'll call you tomorrow" should be viewed as a commitment that God expects us to keep.

Let Your Yes Be Yes

Let your Yes be simply Yes, and your No be simply No; anything more than that comes from the evil one.   *Matthew 5:37*

There was a time not too far in the past when a man's word was his bond. It represented his honor, and not to keep one's word was unthinkable. When people made a business deal, a twenty-page contract covering every minute thing imaginable was not necessary. They simply came to an agreement and shook hands. It is amazing how far we have fallen. Now we have elaborate contracts, and even then if they are broken, we often find there is nothing we can do about it.

We built and moved into a new home about five years ago. It was to be a community with 165 homes, and many promises were given regarding the fine community it would be. Shortly after moving into our home, we were informed by some outraged neighbors that the water storage tank for the community held enough water for only 29 homes, not the 165 that were to be built. Somehow the owner of the property had failed to think about irrigation when having the tank built. It should have been a simple fix. He made a mistake and he should have corrected it! But he refused to take responsibility, and a lawsuit against him ensued. After all, one does need water. We would have been willing to dig a well, but the subdivision rules stated that no wells could be installed.

For four years, eighteen of the homeowners, including us, have paid lawyers to deal with the situation while the man responsible has made one excuse after another to secure delays from our judicial system. In my opinion, none of these delays should have been granted. He should have simply been told to fix the problem without delay. However, since it is commonplace today for people not to keep their word, that didn't happen. One hundred years ago, a situation like this would have been unheard of. But today literally hundreds of thousands of lawsuits are filed to try to make people do what they promised to do. It is sad indeed.

Dave and I really enjoy watching British films from the Victorian era. Everyone was so proper and mannerly, and of course, not being a man or a woman of one's word was unthinkable. We like to say, "We have come a long way, baby," and so we have, but have we gone forward, as we like to think, or are we actually in a dangerous moral downhill slide? We have many problems in our world today, so you might be tempted to think that a small thing like doing what you say you will do is minor compared to the rest of our problems. I beg to differ. I believe that diminished integrity is the source of many other serious problems. Integrity is one of the bedrocks of living the way God wants us to. Not only that, but it makes our lives a lot less complicated! Just think—no more dreading to hear the phone ring with someone following up on a commitment you didn't keep.

Integrity is being honest and doing the right thing in every situation. We cannot make others do what is right, but each of us is responsible to God and ourselves to do right. We must never be the kind of person who says, "Everyone else does it, so what's the big problem?" Even if nobody in the whole world kept their word, we should still keep ours, simply because it is the right thing to do.

Loose Mouth Disease

People with what I call "loose mouth disease" are those who say all kinds of things, including making commitments, without giving one sincere thought to what they are saying. They merely love to talk and they do it incessantly.

> Put away from you false and dishonest speech, and will-ful and contrary talk put far from you.   *Proverbs 4:24*

When we say something that we don't mean, it may be minor to us, but in God's eyes, we have not told the truth.

I am guilty of having had loose mouth disease and being

corrected by God about it, and it is the way I learned the importance of what I am sharing with you. I recall once loosely saying to a couple that we met in Florida, "You should come to St. Louis [where I live] sometime and stay with us a few days. We will show you our city." I came home and thought no more about it, but they remembered and a few months later called and asked when they could come. My first thought was, "I have to find a way to get out of this, because the last thing I want to do right now is have company." I said I would call them back and got busy preparing my list of excuses that I intended to give them when God interrupted my plan. He dealt with me very seriously about the need to keep my word, and not to say things loosely that I had not even given any real thought to. He showed me that I needed to have them come, and do what I said I would and show them the city. He showed me that it would teach me a lesson and I would think twice before saying something like that in the future.

The family did come, and I did learn a lesson, but it wasn't the last time I would need to be refreshed in learning the importance of keeping my word. I try to be careful even when I say something like, "Let's get together for lunch soon," or, "I'll call you next week and we can catch up." The truth is, we often say things like that to people to get rid of them, and we have no intention of seeing them or calling them for lunch. Once you make a serious commitment to God to always do what you say you will do if at all possible, you will be more careful what you say.

A meaningless comment we make can easily be taken as a promise by the listener. I once hurt a friend deeply in a situation just like this. I said something to her that she took as a long-term commitment, and at the time I thought that would be the case. But later God led me in a different direction, and she was wounded. I felt terrible that I didn't act more wisely, and I have learned to say, "We will do this unless God leads us in a different direction." That was what I meant when speaking with her, but I didn't actually say it. I hate nothing more than hurting people, and I have learned that I often do when I have "loose mouth disease."

> In a multitude of words transgression is not lacking, but
> he who restrains his lips is prudent.   *Proverbs 10:19*

You may be thinking of many things by now that you have told people you would do and have never followed through on. There is no point in being condemned, but I do suggest that if they are things you can still do, that it would be good to do them. If not, you might at least call and ask for forgiveness! Ouch! I am sure that doesn't sound very exciting, but it is the right thing to do.

If we take what God's Word says about the words we speak, then we will have to take this subject of "keeping our word" seriously. We can cause ourselves huge problems simply by not being faithful in this area.

> He who guards his mouth keeps his life, but he who
> opens wide his lips comes to ruin.   *Proverbs 13:3*

I like to think of wisdom as doing now what I will be satisfied with later. This means that I cannot make emotional decisions, but I must think about any action before I take it. "The mind of the wise instructs his mouth" (Proverbs 16:23). Are you letting wisdom instruct your mouth, or just talking and not even paying much attention to what you're saying?

Here are a few things I have either been convicted of personally, or have had someone do to me and have learned not to repeat them:

1. If you say you will show up for a volunteer workday at church, show up! It is easy to sign up, but showing up takes more than talk.
2. If you RSVP that you will be at a wedding reception, baby shower, or some other type of party, be sure you either go, or call and cancel your reservation if you cannot go. The people giving the party are ordering food based on your commitment, and it is not showing integrity not to care if they waste their money.
3. If you tell someone you will call back, do it!
4. If you tell someone you will send her something, be sure you send it! I meet people who have needs and often feel that I should send them a certain book. As soon as I tell them I will do so, I call my office and make the arrangements so I don't forget it. "I forgot" is a good excuse, but we should take precaution not to forget.
5. Pay your bills when you say you will pay them, and if for some reason you cannot, then call and make proper arrangements. I once heard a statistic that said churches are worse than anyone about not paying their bills. What a terrible example to set for the world. Of

course, not all churches are like that, but not even one should be.

6. If you are a public speaker and you have committed to an engagement, don't cancel just because you get a better offer. Keeping your word should be more important than a better opportunity.

7. If you own a company, or have authority in a company, and you tell an employee he will get a raise in a year, then be sure to follow through before the year is up. If you let it go three months overdue, it may mean nothing to you, but he is probably sitting on the edge of his seat waiting to hear from you. Do what you would want someone else to do for you.

8. If you commit to have a project done at a certain time, then finish it. If for some reason it is impossible to do so, then call before the promised deadline and ask for an extension.

9. Never tell your children you will do something and then not do it, unless you have a very good reason and explain yourself thoroughly. If we don't do what we tell our children we will do, we can hardly expect them to be truthful with us.

These are all things that are really just common sense, but I find that common sense is not very common anymore.

Have you ever told someone you would do something and then the next time you saw them, you found yourself feeling uncomfortable and making excuses? You can avoid that trouble by practicing wisdom, thinking before you speak, and guarding your mouth.

He who guards his mouth and his tongue keeps himself
from troubles.   *Proverbs 21:23*

It Is Okay to Say "No"

Perhaps a fear of saying "no" to people is one of the reasons
why we make commitments that we don't keep. It is true
that everyone who makes a request wants to hear "yes," but
we all know that just isn't possible. I would rather someone
be unhappy with me because I said "no," than to have him
unhappy because I said "yes" and didn't keep my word.

A well-known pastor recently told me that he frequently
has people from his congregation ask if they can have lunch
with him the next week, and he says, "No." He then goes on
to explain that it is not possible for him to have lunch with
all the members of his congregation and fulfill his duties as
pastor, but he assures them that there are well-qualified people who can meet any need they may have. He told me that
he has discovered that when people genuinely want help, it
does not have to be the pastor who helps them, but on the
other hand, if they simply want him to pay attention to them,
then they frequently are offended.

Many people don't have the courage to say "no." They don't
want to hurt people, or make them angry, so they either say
"yes," not intending to follow through, or they make excuses
that are not based on truth. We should follow the leading of
the Holy Spirit and say "no" when we believe that is what we
are supposed to do, and say "yes" only when we believe that
is what we are supposed to do. We are responsible for being

obedient to God, not keeping everyone in the world happy by doing everything they want us to do. This was a difficult lesson for me to learn, but if I hadn't learned it, I might not still be in ministry today. I would have burned out mentally, emotionally, and physically trying to do all the things that everyone else thought I should do.

Quite often when people ask us to do things, they are not thinking of the impact that their request has on us. They simply want us to do something for them, and that is as far as their thinking goes. It is good to do things for people and to seek to make them happy, but if we feel we never have permission to say "no," it can be disastrous.

I am giving you permission to say "no." God has already given you permission, but just in case you missed it in His Word, I am confirming it for you: IT IS OKAY TO SAY "NO"!

CHAPTER 21

Watch Your Mouth

Learn this and you'll get along, no matter what your station:
An ounce of keep-your-mouth-shut beats a ton of explanation.
—Unknown

There are a few more areas regarding being careful what we say that come to my heart to discuss with you. As we have said, words can heal, but they can also injure. They can build up or tear down. They can encourage or discourage. They can open a door of blessing in our own lives, or they can open a door of destruction.

I have purpose that my mouth shall not transgress.   *Psalm 17:3b*

Coarse Jesting

The apostle Paul wrote a letter to the church at Ephesus, and in it he urged them not to engage in foolish and silly talk, or coarse jesting. Jesting is something done for amusement, or something said in a joking manner. We all enjoy humorous people, but we don't enjoy being the source of their humor, especially if they are making a joke based on one of our flaws or shortcomings. It might even be funny once, but if continued over and over, it almost always causes offense.

We have all had our feelings hurt by someone who was simply trying to be funny, and we more than likely have all hurt someone else's feelings while trying to be funny. I think the best policy is to be especially careful when teasing people about any mistake they have made, any negative trait they have, or anything about them personally that is unusual. Never tease overweight people about their weight, bald men about their baldness, or extremely tall or short people about their height. I can assure you that they are sensitive about these areas, and even if they laugh with you, it may hurt them deep inside.

I know a man who is naturally very humorous, and when I am around him, I laugh and laugh, but I have never heard him be rude to anyone in order to get a laugh. If we have to make fun of other people to be funny, then we are not truly funny—just rude. Truly funny people usually don't need to "try" to be funny—they just are—and half the time they don't even know it. Like any gift that God gives us, it flows naturally without much effort. I believe some people are anointed or gifted by God to bring laughter to others, but they still need to use wisdom.

I use examples in my preaching about Dave frequently, and I try to be very careful not to sound rude or disrespectful. But a couple of times I have said things that have hurt his feelings, and I can always tell when I do. I quickly and profusely apologize because the last thing I ever want to do is hurt someone while I am preaching God's Word.

Don't ever try to get a laugh at someone else's expense. Even people who are very secure don't like to be teased about their flaws. My voice is unusually deep for a woman and I truly am not insecure about it, but if someone kept teasing me about it, I am sure it would make me uncomfortable.

Not too long ago Dave made a mistake about something (thankfully, I don't remember what it was), and I teased him about it in front of some other people. Immediately I knew that I had done the wrong thing. I was trying to be funny, but he felt embarrassed and belittled. A woman should have better sense than to tease her husband about a mistake he made, because it is just not wise! If we say anything, it should be, "Honey, it was no big deal. I make mistakes worse than that all the time."

I watched a movie last night that had a good example of what I am talking about. Robert and Emma were at a party and someone asked Emma why she and Robert were not dancing. She replied without hesitation, "Robert doesn't dance well, and he won't do anything if he can't do it well because it would hurt his pride."

Emma thought no more about her comment, and in her mind she was merely teasing, but Robert continued to think about it. The next day he told Emma that she had embarrassed him in front of their friends and made him feel belittled. She said, "Oh, Robert, I was only teasing." Robert replied, "No, you weren't teasing, you were letting me and our friends know that you think I am filled with pride, and it hurt me." There are times when we use "I am only joking" as an excuse to tell people things that we feel about them but don't have the courage to discuss with them in a proper way. We should always be straightforward in our speech and never say things with hidden meaning.

Don't Make a Joke out of Something That God Doesn't Think Is Funny!

Talk shows are very popular today. The name is accurate, because all they do is "talk," but they rarely say anything that is truly worth listening to. In fact, frequently they simply make fun of people. I think we are all guilty at times of laughing at things that God does not think are funny at all.

I don't think public officials should be made fun of, and it happens frequently on talk shows. Even if we don't like them, we should not make fun of them. Pray for them, but don't make jokes about their wrong behavior. The results of their wrong choices are not funny for the nation, and they aren't something to be made light of. Now you might be thinking, "Oh, come on, Joyce, lighten up. People are just trying to have fun." But all you have to do is ask yourself how you would feel if you were the one being made fun of. You would not like it, and neither would I. Remember the Golden Rule: "Do unto others as you would have them do unto you."

Don't Use the Lord's Name in Vain

Using God's name in vain is much more than attaching it to a curse word like *damn*. It means to use it uselessly or frivolously.

> You shall not use or repeat the name of the Lord your God in vain [that is, lightly or frivolously, in false affirmations or profanely]; for the Lord will not hold him guiltless who takes His name in vain.   *Exodus 20:7*

We hear the names "God" or "Jesus" used frequently and often by people who have no relationship with Him at all. Statements like "Oh, my God" are repeated often on television shows in ways that have absolutely no sincerity behind them at all. "For Christ's sake" is another frequently used statement, when what is taking place has nothing to do with Christ at all. Did you ever wonder why God's name is used so often in a world where many people claim not to even believe He exists? I have, and I think it is evidence that perhaps they believe more than they would care to admit.

I frequently am around Christians who say, "Oh, my God," when they are surprised by something, or even if they look outside and a lot of snow is on the ground. I think we need to be more sincere in how we use God's name. Honor His name by using it when you are genuinely calling on Him in prayer, praise, or worship, but never lightly or frivolously.

Telling the Truth

When the judicial court system first began requiring witnesses to lay their hand on the Bible and confess, "I promise to tell the truth, the whole truth, and nothing but the truth, so help me God," people lived in very different times. They were times when the truth was very important to most people. The courts still do that today, but few people even realize or care what they are saying, and it is sad. Lying is quite common today. Adults do it in front of their children and then get angry when their children lie to them.

Have you ever told your child to tell someone on the phone that you weren't home simply because you didn't feel like talking? If so, you encouraged your child to lie. Have you ever called your place of employment and said you couldn't come to work because you were sick, when the truth was that you simply wanted to do something else that day? Have you been late for an appointment and made the excuse that you got stuck in heavy traffic, when the truth was that you didn't leave home when you should have? Children often lie to keep from getting into trouble, and adults often do the same thing. One of the Ten Commandments is "Thou shalt not bear false witness." In other words: "Do not lie." So telling the truth, even when it hurts, must be very important to God.

Someone told me a secret once and asked me not to tell anyone else. I said that I would not, but I did. She found out and asked me if I was the one who told, and I quickly said "no," because I didn't want to ruin our friendship. As soon as

I hung up the phone, the Holy Spirit convicted me that I had told a lie, and He didn't let up until I finally called the person back and told her the truth. That incident was so embarrassing to me that I will never forget it, and it taught me a good lesson. We absolutely cannot lie and think it is okay. There is no such thing as a "little white lie." A lie is a lie, and God commands us to always tell the truth.

The Bible mentions seven things that the Lord hates, and a lying tongue is one of them (see Proverbs 6:16–19).

> For my mouth shall utter truth, and wrongdoing is detestable and loathsome to my lips.
>
> All the words of my mouth are righteous (upright and in right standing with God); there is nothing contrary to truth or crooked in them. *Proverbs 8:7–8*

Satan is known as the Deceiver; he is a liar and the father of all lies, and the truth is not in him (see John 8:44). God, on the other hand, is Truth. Jesus said, "I am The Way, The truth, and The Life, no man comes to the Father but by me" (John 14:6). Satan lies to all of us, and the only way we can recognize and resist his lies is to know God's Word, which is truth!

Living Truly

We can lie and not even open our mouth—by saying we believe one thing and living in an entirely different way. When we do that our lives are lies. The apostle John said

that if we say we know God and don't keep His commandments, then we are liars (see 1 John 2:22). He also said that
if we say we love God and we hate our brothers in Christ,
then we are liars (see 1 John 4:20). Not only do our lives lie
when we do such things, but we are lying to ourselves, and
there is no worse deception than self-deception. For many
years I thought I knew and loved God, yet I was angry at
someone for something most of the time. I was deceived, and
the fruit of the deception was evident in my life. I had no
peace, no joy, no real success, constant financial need, and
was confused about "why" I had those problems.

We learn truth by learning God's Word. We live truth by
making every effort to live according to God's Word, and
when we fail, we admit it (tell the truth) and ask God to forgive us. And we should all be totally committed to telling the
truth in every situation, even if doing so causes us personal
trouble or embarrassment.

Be Careful What You Hate

The word *hate* means "a passionate and fervent dislike." It
is a feeling so strong that it often moves a person to hostile
actions. If we are going to hate anything, we must be sure we
hate what God hates—and that is evil and all wickedness.
God commands us not to hate even our enemies, but to love
and pray for them. From the beginning of time starting with
Cain and Abel, men have hated one another, and it has only
caused killing, wars, violence, and wickedness of every kind.

How often do you say that you hate a thing? Don't say

things like, "I hate the weather, I hate my job, I hate my hair, I hate my neighborhood, I hate my automobile"—and especially don't ever say that you hate another person.

The more we speak a thing out of our mouth, the more of it we have. Talking about hate will only increase the feelings of hate in your life. Some people make the mistake of hating their life, when they should embrace it and make the best of it that they can. Hating our life won't change it, but it does change us. It makes us bitter, resentful, and jealous. We always think we want what someone else has, but we fail to realize that they may want what we have. Very few people learn the blessed lesson of loving the life they have and never comparing themselves or what they have to anyone else.

If you dislike something in your life, then change it if you can. If you don't like your job, then look for a different one. If you don't like your neighborhood, then move. If you don't like the weather, you can't change it, so change your attitude. Change what you can and have the wisdom to know what you can't change. Learn to love everything except evil. The more you are filled with loving thoughts and the more you speak loving words, the happier you will be.

Saying that you hate things may just be a habit you have formed. It's a way of expressing your displeasure with something, but does it do you any good? Of course it doesn't. You can spend your entire life hating first one thing and then another, and it will never make your life better.

If you have hated your daily drive to work in traffic, be determined to find a way to enjoy it. Carpool with someone you enjoy, play music, pray, or listen to instructional CDs and use the time to educate yourself. I met a woman a couple of days ago who mentioned that she drives one and a half hours each way to work. I asked her if she disliked it and she said, "The drive is beautiful and I love the place I work and the people I work with." She gave the perfect answer and what she said even made me happy. Many people would have said, "I hate the drive, I am so tired of doing it twice every day, the job is not worth it, and the people irritate me," but all they would have done is make themselves more miserable.

I encourage you to begin to verbalize that you like, enjoy, and love things. The more you say it, the more you will feel it.

Eliminate the Word *Worry* from Your Vocabulary

I wonder how many times the statement "I'm worried that . . ." goes out into the atmosphere? Millions of people use this phrase possibly millions of times throughout their lives, but what is the use of it? It is vain, powerless, and useless, and it doesn't help us in any way.

If someone asked you, "Do you think worrying will change your situation?" I am sure you would say "no," so why keep doing it? Worry never changes anything, but us. Start listening to yourself and other people, and each time you hear "I'm worried," say to yourself, "That is a useless statement." If we thoroughly realize the foolishness of it, maybe we will stop saying it.

People say things like, *I am worried about retirement, I am worried about my children, I am worried I might go bald like my dad did, I am worried about layoffs at work, I am worried about the world economy, I am worried about gaining weight, I am worried about getting old,* and all kinds of other useless statements. Don't worry about retirement, but instead plan ahead and retirement can be peaceful. Don't worry about gaining weight, but just eat right and exercise. Don't worry about anything, but pray instead. Pray right away and don't delay!

Mere worry immobilizes us; we sit and worry and do very little of anything that might help our situation. Worry disempowers us! It steals our peace and joy and makes us age faster. Some people feel they are obligated to worry and say silly things like, "I can't help it, I am just a worrier." Of course we can help it; otherwise God would not have told us not to worry.

Instead of saying, "I'm worried," replace those negative useless words with, "I trust God." When we say that we trust God, it releases His power to work in our lives. When we say that we are worried, it hinders Him. Even if you tend to worry, stop saying it. Study God's Word, remember His faithfulness to you in past situations, and be determined to stop wasting your time worrying.

God's will is for us to have the best lives possible, but that is impossible unless we learn the power of words and say those things that benefit us.

type of a

CHAPTER
22

Do You Want to Change Your Life?

Our words belong to us, and we must be responsible for how we use them. Perhaps if we view words differently, then we will use them in a better way. They are valuable, they are containers for power, and they can produce life or death for us and for all who hear them. They are a gift from God, and when used properly, they are one of our greatest assets. We have hundreds of thousands of words floating around inside our hearts and heads all day long, and we must choose carefully which ones we speak. Most of us have probably spent many years if not our entire lives simply talking without even thinking. Some people say, "I am the type of person who speaks my mind," but that does not make the person wise or pleasant to be with.

If you use your words wisely, then I congratulate you, but if you don't, then I urge you to begin asking God to help you and start making changes right away. The more you improve the way you talk, the more your life will improve.

Since words contain the power of life and death (see Proverbs 18:21), when we speak wrong ones, we are committing spiritual suicide. When we speak right ones, we are blessing ourselves and filling our lives and the atmosphere we are in with life, and life more abundant!

Facts or Truth?

One of the best ways to have a mouth filled with wisdom is to always speak truth instead of merely speaking facts. God's Word is truth and it will prevail over the facts (circumstances) in our life if we release it through speaking.

What are some of the facts in your life right now that you really want to see changed? How have you been talking about them? Do you speak as if they will always be that way, or do you speak God's Word to the mountains in your life and tell them to move? If you have said the right thing, how often have you said it? Are you persistent in speaking God's Word concerning your life? Persistence always pays off. We should never get weary in doing what is right because we will reap in due season.

I have already shared the importance of speaking God's Word in other parts of this book, but I must reemphasize it. Talking about what we think, see, and feel is one of the easiest traps to fall into. The things we see and feel are so real to us, and we consider them to be the truth of what is happening in our lives. But they are not the truth; they are the facts, and facts can change, but truth never changes. Jesus is the same yesterday, today, and forever. He changes not, but He is able to change anything in our lives that need changing.

In order to see God's power manifested in our lives in amazing ways, we need to come into agreement with Him and say what He says. I want you to be filled with the hope of change because hopelessness is a miserable place to be. I have had a lot of dental work done lately and one tooth has been painful since the day it was worked on, and that was almost five months ago. Two different dentists have told me that they see nothing wrong with the tooth so I am continuing every day to hope that it will be better that day and I say, "Every day my tooth gets better." Guess what! It has improved and I have been out of bed four hours today and it hasn't hurt yet! Sometimes things just take time, and we can cooperate with the process of healing in any area of our lives by staying positive and speaking words of hope and faith.

Even if the words don't change your circumstances right away, they will change you into a more pleasant and joyful individual. Talking about our problems only increases anxiety.

How to Respond to Negative Words from Other People

Learning not to be negative ourselves and to be careful about the words we speak does not prevent other people from saying things to us that either hurt us, or try to hinder our progress. We can listen to them and believe what they say, or we can look to God's Word (the truth) and believe what He says.

The following story is humorous, but it also reveals an important truth that we all can learn from:

A group of frogs were traveling through the woods, and two of them fell into a deep pit. All the other frogs gathered around the pit. When they saw how deep the pit was, they told the two frogs that they were as good as dead.

The two frogs ignored the comments and tried to jump up out of the pit with all their might. The other frogs kept telling them to stop, that they were as good as dead. Finally, one of the frogs took heed to what the other frogs were saying and gave up. He fell down and died.

The other frog continued to jump as hard as he could. Once again, the crowd of frogs yelled at him to stop the pain and just die. He jumped even harder and finally made it out. When he got out, the other frogs said, "Did you not hear us?" The frog explained to them that he was deaf. He thought they were encouraging him the entire time.

Although none of us would want to be deaf, there are times when we need to act as if we were. It would be amazing what people would be able to do with their lives if they only believed they could. We must not let the negative words of others affect us, because it is not their opinion that matters in the end. The important thing is what God says about us in His Word, and what we believe about ourselves.

A ruler of the synagogue named Jairus came to Jesus and asked him to come and lay His hands on his sick daughter so she might be healed. As Jesus was going with him, another woman who also needed healing stopped Jesus, and he took time to minister to her. While they were stopped, servants from Jairus' house came and said that his daughter had died and there was no need to bother Jesus any further. But look at Jesus' response to that report:

Overhearing but ignoring what they said, Jesus said to
the ruler of the synagogue, Do not be seized with alarm
and struck with fear; only keep on believing.   *Mark 5:36*

I have always loved that verse because it helps me remember that there are times when we absolutely must not listen to the negative things that people tell us. The frog got out of the pit because he believed he could. It was to his advantage that he could not hear the other frogs repeatedly telling him to stop trying and just die. His perception became his reality. He believed he could get out of the pit and he did. You can also get out of any pit you may find yourself in if you will only listen to God's Word, and never to anyone who speaks words of defeat and failure to you.

Have you missed opportunities in your own life to do great things because you have listened too intently to the words of others? If so, it is still not too late. You can begin this very moment erasing the memories of negative words spoken to you by confessing God's Word about you and your future out loud until it becomes a reality in your life.

You can defeat every negative thought that comes to your mind, and every negative statement made to you, by wielding the sword of the Spirit, which is the Word of God. To wield it means to use it, speak it, meditate on it, believe it, and let it guide all your actions.

For the Word that God speaks is alive and full of power
[making it active, operative, energizing, and effective];
it is sharper than any two-edged sword, penetrating
to the dividing line of the breath of life (soul) and [the

immortal] spirit, and of joints and marrow [of the deepest parts of our nature], exposing and sifting and analyzing and judging the very thoughts and purposes of the heart.   *Hebrews 4:12*

Let's say for example that you are working on a project with several other people, and absolutely nothing has gone the way you expected. Every day there has been some kind of problem that has caused you more work than you originally anticipated. Along with everyone else, you are becoming tired and weary. Your thinking is getting more and more negative: "This is never going to work. I just cannot finish this job; it is too difficult." Then the people working with you start saying that they want to quit and consider the project to be a lost cause. Deep in your heart you believe you should finish the task, but in order for that to happen, you will need to respond to your own negative thoughts and the negative words of others. You can do that by wielding the sword of the Spirit. By speaking portions of God's Word that address your unique situation, you can say things like this:

- I can do all things through Christ, Who gives me strength. (Philippians 4:13)
- I am strong in the Lord and the power of His might; I draw my strength from Him. (Ephesians 6:10)
- I am not moved by these problems and I will finish what I have started. (Acts 20:24)
- I am rooted, established, strong, immovable, and determined about this project. (1 Peter 5:9)

These scriptures and others like them will empower you to follow your heart instead of your mind and the words of other people. God's Word is only valuable to us as we believe it, speak it, and take action accordingly.

I never understood the power of words until I experienced the power of God's Word working in my own life. I can honestly say that learning, and believing, and speaking God's Word changed me, and my entire approach to life. God's Word has power inherent in it, and when released, the power explodes into amazing enabling ability. Think of God's Word like this: You have an enemy attacking, and in your hand you hold a grenade. All you have to do is pull the pin and throw the grenade. You have the equipment you need to defeat your enemies, and surely you would not stand idle and watch your life being destroyed. However, many Christians do just that. They have the Word of God, the equipment needed to defeat their enemies, and yet they stand silent. Silence is agreement, so if we refuse to open our mouths and speak God's Word, then we are agreeing with our circumstances and giving them continued power over us.

If you are like most people, you are going to be saying something, so it might as well be something that could help you.

We cannot prevent people from saying things we would often rather not hear, but we can decide for ourselves if we are going to listen to them and take them seriously. We can decide if we are going to believe what people say above what God has said about us in His Word. Nobody can change your destiny with their words if you don't let them. My father told me repeatedly when I was a young girl that I would never amount to anything. I remember lying in bed at night thinking, "Someday I am going to do something great." It seemed that the more he said I could not succeed, the more determined I was to prove him wrong. Maybe I was just stubborn, but if so, I am grateful, because it prevented me from agreeing with him. Don't agree with anything negative that is said to you or about you.

Just in case you have had a lot of discouraging and negative things said to you, I want to reverse the damage that has been done by saying some good things to you:

- You are a special person, and without you, the world would be missing something wonderful.
- You can do whatever you set your mind to do, as long as it is within God's will.
- You are talented, gifted by God, and you are able to accomplish great things in your life.
- You are amazingly unique, and you never need to compare yourself with anyone else. Be the amazing person that you are.
- God loves you unconditionally, and that will never change.
- Your future is so bright that you may need sunglasses to look at it!

A Turning Point in Your Life

No matter what your life has been like until now, I pray that you will make reading this book a turning point for you. As you apply the principles throughout the book, you will see positive changes. You may be thinking, "I wish I had known all these principles twenty years ago." That probably would have been good, but you do know them now, so don't waste one more day. Beginning today, let your words work for you rather than against you. It will take diligence and you won't reach perfection immediately, but be thankful that you know the pathway to victory now.

I am on a journey myself to only use my words for things that will be beneficial to me or others. While you are making your own personal journey, you can remember that I am right there with you still growing and learning.

I recognize the Holy Spirit's conviction much quicker now when I say something that I should not say, but I don't let it condemn me. I am thankful that I am more sensitive to the power of my words, and I welcome all the correction that God gives me. I do pray that you will not feel condemned every time you make a mistake, because it will only weaken you and cause you to make even more mistakes. Conviction is never intended to condemn us, but to help us admit our mistakes—ask for and receive God's forgiveness and press on to the next level of victory.

Here is a good confession to make daily about your words:

I don't allow any corrupt communication to go out of my mouth, but I only speak what is good, uplifting and edifying (see Ephesians 4:29).

I am careful about what I say and I don't sin with my tongue (see Psalm 39:1). I keep my tongue and my soul from trouble (see Proverbs 21:23). My tongue is gentle and full of healing power (see Proverbs 15:4). I speak excellent things and open my mouth for right things. I always speak truth and nothing perverse comes out of my mouth (see Proverbs 8:6–8). I open my mouth with wisdom, and the law of kindness is in my tongue (see Proverbs 31:26). My conversation is filled with grace and love, and I know how to answer every person (see Colossians 4:6).

I encourage you to read the Book of Proverbs and highlight every passage that talks about the mouth, our words, or the tongue. Once you do, you can go through Proverbs and get a quick refresher course on the power of words just by reading what you have highlighted.

I am really excited for you because I know how changing your words will change your life. Enjoy your journey and remember to thank God for every little bit of progress that you make. No man can tame the tongue, so pray daily and ask for God's help in making sure the words of your mouth and the meditations of your heart are acceptable in His sight.

APPENDIX

A Dictionary of God's Word

God's Word is the most powerful thing on earth. In the beginning, He said, "Let there be light, and there was." I urge you to respect and value God's Word as the greatest treasure you have.

God has exalted His name and His Word above all else, and He has exalted His Word even above all of His name (see Psalm 138:2). As you learn God's Word, believe it, meditate on it, and speak it, you will be changed.

As we continue in God's Word, we are changed into His image in ever-increasing degrees of glory (see 2 Corinthians 3:18). God's Word changes us! We must expect to *continue* in it. That means we must live, dwell, and remain in it. Reading one book or memorizing a few scriptures about the power of words won't be enough to make permanent changes in your life. You will need to make a lifetime commitment to studying and living by the Word of God.

The Word of God is practical and can be applied to your life every day. I want to leave you with a small dictionary of God's Word that you can speak when certain situations arise in your life. I hope you will add to it and use it daily.

When you feel that you don't have the strength to go on

- I have strength for all things in Christ, Who empowers me. I am ready for anything and equal to anything through Him Who infuses inner strength into me; I am self-sufficient in Christ's sufficiency. (Philippians 4:13)
- The Lord is my Shepherd [to feed, guide, and shield me], I shall not lack.

  He makes me lie down in [fresh, tender] green pastures; He leads me beside the still and restful waters.

  He refreshes and restores my life (my self); He leads me in the paths of righteousness [uprightness and right standing with Him—not for my earning it, but] for His name's sake.

  Yes, though I walk through the [deep, sunless] valley of the shadow of death, I will fear or dread no evil, for You are with me; Your rod [to protect] and Your staff [to guide], they comfort me. You prepare a table before me in the presence of my enemies. You anoint my head with oil; my [brimming] cup runs over. Surely or only goodness, mercy, and unfailing love shall follow me all the days of my life, and through the length of my days the house of the Lord [and His presence] shall be my dwelling place. (Psalm 23)
- Therefore I tell you, stop being perpetually uneasy (anxious and worried) about your life, what you shall eat or what you shall drink; or about your body, what you shall put on. Is not life greater [in quality] than food, and the body [far above and more excellent] than clothing?

  Look at the birds of the air; they neither sow nor reap nor gather into barns, and yet your heavenly Father keeps feeding them. Are you not worth much more than they?

And who of you by worrying and being anxious can add one unit of measure (cubit) to his stature or to the span of his life?

And why should you be anxious about clothes? Consider the lilies of the field and learn thoroughly how they grow; they neither toil nor spin.

Yet I tell you, even Solomon in all his magnificence (excellence, dignity, and grace) was not arrayed like one of these.

But if God so clothes the grass of the field, which today is alive and green and tomorrow is tossed into the furnace, will He not much more surely clothe you, O you of little faith?

Therefore do not worry and be anxious, saying, What are we going to have to eat? or, What are we going to have to drink? or, What are we going to have to wear?

For the Gentiles (heathen) wish for and crave and diligently seek all these things, and your heavenly Father knows well that you need them all.

But seek (aim at and strive after) first of all His kingdom and His righteousness (His way of doing and being right), and then all these things taken together will be given you besides. (Matthew 6: 25–33)

When you are angry and bitter

- Cease from anger and forsake wrath; fret not yourself—it tends only to evildoing. (Psalm 37:8)

- The Lord is merciful and gracious, slow to anger and plenteous in mercy and loving-kindness. (Psalm 103:8)
- He who is slow to anger has great understanding, but he who is hasty of spirit exposes and exalts his folly. (Proverbs 14:29)
- A soft answer turns away wrath, but grievous words stir up anger. (Proverbs 15:1)
- A hot-tempered man stirs up strife, but he who is slow to anger appeases contention. (Proverbs 15:18)
- Good sense makes a man restrain his anger, and it is his glory to overlook a transgression or an offense. (Proverbs 19:11)
- Do not be quick in spirit to be angry or vexed, for anger and vexation lodge in the bosom of fools. (Ecclesiastes 7:9)
- When angry, do not sin; do not ever let your wrath (your exasperation, your fury or indignation) last until the sun goes down. (Ephesians 4:26)
- Let all bitterness and indignation and wrath (passion, rage, bad temper) and resentment (anger, animosity) and quarreling (brawling, clamor, contention) and slander (evil-speaking, abusive, or blasphemous language) be banished from you, with all malice (spite, ill will, or baseness of any kind). And become useful and helpful and kind to one another, tenderhearted (compassionate, understanding, loving-hearted), forgiving one another [readily and freely], as God in Christ forgave you. (Ephesians 4:31–32)
- But now put away and rid yourselves [completely] of all these things: anger, rage, bad feeling toward others,

curses and slander, and foulmouthed abuse and shameful utterances from your lips! (Colossians 3:8)

- Understand [this], my beloved brethren. Let every man be quick to hear [a ready listener], slow to speak, slow to take offense and to get angry. For man's anger does not promote the righteousness God [wishes and requires]. (James 1:19–20)

When you need confidence

- Have I not commanded you? Be strong, vigorous, and very courageous. Be not afraid, neither be dismayed, for the Lord your God is with you wherever you go. (Joshua 1:9)

- For by You I can run through a troop, and by my God I can leap over a wall. (Psalm 18:29)

- Trust (lean on, rely on, and be confident) in the Lord and do good; so shall you dwell in the land and feed surely on His faithfulness, and truly you shall be fed. (Psalm 37:3)

- My heart is fixed, O God, my heart is steadfast and confident! I will sing and make melody. (Psalm 57:7)

- O Lord of hosts, blessed (happy, fortunate, to be envied) is the man who trusts in You [leaning and believing on You, committing all and confidently looking to You, and that without fear or misgiving]! (Psalm 84:12)

- The fear of man brings a snare, but whoever leans on, trusts in, and puts his confidence in the Lord is safe and set on high. (Proverbs 29:25)

- You will guard him and keep him in perfect and constant peace whose mind [both its inclination and its character] is stayed on You, because he commits himself to You, leans on You, and hopes confidently in You. (Isaiah 26:3)

- For thus said the Lord God, the Holy One of Israel. In returning [to Me] and resting [in Me] you shall be saved; in quietness and in [trusting] confidence shall be your strength. (Isaiah 30:15)

- But as for me, I will look to the Lord and confident in Him I will keep watch; I will wait with hope and expectancy for the God of my salvation; my God will hear me. (Micah 7:7)

- And I am convinced and sure of this very thing, that He Who began a good work in you will continue until the day of Jesus Christ [right up to the time of His return], developing [that good work] and perfecting and bringing it to full completion in you. (Philippians 1:6)

- For we [Christians] are the true circumcision, who worship God in spirit and by the Spirit of God and exult and glory and pride ourselves in Jesus Christ, and put no confidence or dependence [on what we are] in the flesh and on outward privileges and physical advantages and external appearances. (Philippians 3:3)

- Let us then fearlessly and confidently and boldly draw near to the throne of grace (the throne of God's unmerited favor to us sinners), that we may receive mercy [for our failures] and find grace to help in good time for every need [appropriate help and well-timed help, coming just when we need it]. (Hebrews 4:16)

- Do not, therefore, fling away your fearless confidence, for it carries a great and glorious compensation of reward. (Hebrews 10:35)

When you are discouraged

- I have told you these things, so that in Me you may have [perfect] peace and confidence. In the world you have tribulation and trials and distress and frustration; but be of good cheer [take courage; be confident, certain, undaunted]! For I have overcome the world. [I have deprived it of power to harm you and have conquered it for you.] (John 16:33)

- We are assured and know that [God being a partner in their labor] all things work together and are [fitting into a plan] for good to and for those who love God and are called according to [His] design and purpose. (Romans 8:28)

- We are hedged in (pressed) on every side [troubled and oppressed in every way], but not cramped or crushed; we suffer embarrassments and are perplexed and unable to find a way out, but not driven to despair. (2 Corinthians 4:8)

- Therefore we do not become discouraged (utterly spiritless, exhausted, and wearied out through fear). Though our outer man is [progressively] decaying and wasting away, yet our inner self is being [progressively] renewed day after day. For our light, momentary affliction (this slight distress of the passing hour) is ever more and more abundantly preparing and producing and achieving for us an everlasting weight of glory [beyond all measure, excessively surpassing all comparisons and all calculations, a vast and transcendent glory and blessedness never to cease!]. (2 Corinthians 4:16–17)

- But He said to me, My grace (My favor and loving-kindness and mercy) is enough for you [sufficient against any danger and enables you to bear the trouble manfully]; for My strength and power are made perfect (fulfilled and completed) and show themselves most effective in [your] weakness. Therefore, I will all the more gladly glory in my weaknesses and infirmities, that the strength and power of Christ (the Messiah) may rest (yes, may pitch a tent over and dwell) upon me! (2 Corinthians 12:9)

- I have strength for all things in Christ Who empowers me [I am ready for anything and equal to anything through Him Who infuses inner strength into me; I am self-sufficient in Christ's sufficiency]. (Philippians 4:13)

When you are depressed

- It is the Lord Who goes before you; He will [march] with you; He will not fail you or let you go or forsake you; [let there be no cowardice or flinching, but] fear not, neither become broken [in spirit—depressed, dismayed, and unnerved with alarm]. (Deuteronomy 31:8)

- The eyes of the Lord are toward the [uncompromisingly] righteous and His ears are open to their cry. The face of the Lord is against those who do evil, to cut off the remembrance of them from the earth. When the righteous cry for help, the Lord hears, and delivers them out of all their distress and troubles. (Psalm 34:15–17)

- Why are you cast down, O my inner self? And why should you moan over me and be disquieted within me?

Hope in God and wait expectantly for Him, for I shall yet praise Him, my Help and my God. (Psalm 42:5)

- He who dwells in the secret place of the Most High shall remain stable and fixed under the shadow of the Almighty [Whose power no foe can withstand]. I will say of the Lord, He is my Refuge and my Fortress, my God; on Him I lean and rely, and in Him I [confidently] trust! (Psalm 91:1–2)

When you are afraid

- The Lord is my Light and my Salvation—whom shall I fear or dread? The Lord is the Refuge and Stronghold of my life—of whom shall I be afraid? (Psalm 27:1)
- [Then] He will cover you with His pinions, and under His wings shall you trust and find refuge; His truth and His faithfulness are a shield and a buckler. You shall not be afraid of the terror of the night, nor of the arrow (the evil plots and slanders of the wicked) that flies by day. (Psalm 91: 4–5)
- He shall not be afraid of evil tidings; his heart is firmly fixed, trusting (leaning on and being confident) in the Lord. His heart is established and steady, he will not be afraid while he waits to see his desire established upon his adversaries. (Psalm 112:7–8)
- The fear of man brings a snare, but whoever leans on, trusts in, and puts his confidence in the Lord is safe and set on high. (Proverbs 29:25)
- Fear not [there is nothing to fear] for I am with you; do not look around you in terror and be dismayed, for I

am your God. I will strengthen and harden you to difficulties, yes, I will help you; yes, I will hold you up and
retain you with My [victorious] right hand of rightness
and justice. (Isaiah 41:10)

- You shall establish yourself in righteousness (rightness,
in conformity with God's will and order): you shall be
far from even the thought of oppression or destruction,
for you shall not fear, and from terror, for it shall not
come near you. (Isaiah 54:14)

- For [God] Himself has said, I will not in any way fail
you nor give you up nor leave you without support. [I
will] not, [I will] not, [I will] not in any degree leave you
helpless nor forsake nor let [you] down (relax My hold
on you)! [Assuredly not!] So we take comfort and are
encouraged and confidently and boldly say, The Lord is
my Helper; I will not be seized with alarm [I will not
fear or dread or be terrified]. What can man do to me?
(Hebrews 13:5–6)

When you need healing

- He heals the brokenhearted and binds up their wounds
[curing their pains and their sorrows]. (Psalm 147:3)
- Then shall your light break forth like the morning, and
your healing (your restoration and the power of a new
life) shall spring forth speedily; your righteousness
(your rightness, your justice, and your right relationship
with God) shall go before you [conducting you to peace
and prosperity], and the glory of the Lord shall be your
rear guard. (Isaiah 58:8)

- Heal me, O Lord, and I shall be healed; save me, and I shall be saved, for You are my praise. (Jeremiah 17:14)

- For I will restore health to you, and I will heal your wounds, says the Lord, because they have called you an outcast, saying, This is Zion, whom no one seeks after and for whom no one cares! (Jeremiah 30:17)

- Is anyone among you sick? He should call in the church elders (the spiritual guides). And they should pray over him, anointing him with oil in the Lord's name. And the prayer [that is] of faith will save him who is sick, and the Lord will restore him; and if he has committed sins, he will be forgiven. (James 5:14–15)

When you have been abandoned

- Have I not commanded you? Be strong, vigorous, and very courageous. Be not afraid, neither be dismayed, for the Lord your God is with you wherever you go. (Joshua 1:9)

When you have been rejected or betrayed

- Blessed are you when people revile you and persecute you and say all kinds of evil things against you falsely on My account. Be glad and supremely joyful, for your reward in heaven is great (strong and intense), for in this same way people persecuted the prophets who were before you. (Matthew 5: 11–12)

- Behold, I am with you all the days (perpetually, uniformly, and on every occasion), to the [very] close and consummation of the age. Amen (so let it be). (Matthew 28:20)

- But whenever you go into a town and they do not receive and accept and welcome you, go out into its streets and say, Even the dust of your town that clings to our feet we are wiping off against you; yet know and understand this: the kingdom of God has come near you. (Luke 10: 10–11)
- What then shall we say to [all] this? If God is for us, who [can be] against us? [Who can be our foe, if God is on our side?] (Romans 8:31)

When you are lonely

- And behold, I am with you and will keep (watch over you with care, take notice of) you wherever you may go, and I will bring you back to this land; for I will not leave you until I have done all of which I have told you. (Genesis 28:15)
- The Lord will not forsake His people for His great name's sake, for it has pleased Him to make you a people for Himself. (1 Samuel 12:22)
- [Lord] turn to me and be gracious to me, for I am lonely and afflicted. (Psalm 25:16)
- Although my father and my mother have forsaken me, yet the Lord will take me up [adopt me as His child]. (Psalm 27:10)
- God is our Refuge and Strength [mighty and impenetrable to temptation], a very present and well-proved help in trouble. (Psalm 46:1)
- I will not leave you as orphans [comfortless, desolate, bereaved, forlorn, helpless]; I will come [back] to you. (John 14:18)

When you need financial help

- The Lord shall command the blessing upon you in your storehouse and in all that you undertake. And He will bless you in the land which the Lord your God gives you…And the Lord shall make you have a surplus of prosperity, through the fruit of your body, of your livestock, and of your ground, in the land which the Lord swore to your fathers to give you. (Deuteronomy 28:8, 11)

- The young lions lack food and suffer hunger, but they who seek (inquire of and require) the Lord [by right of their need and on the authority of His Word], none of them shall lack any beneficial thing. (Psalm 34:10)

- Bring all the tithes (the whole tenth of your income) into the storehouse, that there may be food in My house, and prove Me now by it, says the Lord of hosts, if I will not open the windows of heaven for you and pour you out a blessing, that there shall not be room enough to receive it. (Malachi 3:10)

- Keep out of debt and owe no man anything, except to love one another; for he who loves his neighbor [who practices loving others] has fulfilled the Law [relating to one's fellowmen, meeting all its requirements]. (Romans 13:8)

- And my God will liberally supply (fill to the full) your every need according to His riches in glory in Christ Jesus. (Philippians 4:19)

- Acquaint now yourself with Him [agree with God and show yourself to be conformed to His will] and be at

peace; by that [you shall prosper and great] good shall
come to you. (Job 22:21)

When you have lost your joy

- For in the day of trouble He will hide me in His shelter;
  in the secret place of His tent will He hide me; He will
  set me high upon a rock. (Psalm 27:5)
- My soul, wait only upon God and silently submit to
  Him; for my hope and expectation are from Him. He
  only is my Rock and my Salvation; He is my Defense and
  my Fortress; I shall not be moved. (Psalm 62:5–6)
- This is my comfort and consolation in my affliction: that
  Your word has revived me and given me life. (Psalm 119:50)
- Though I walk in the midst of trouble, You will revive
  me; You will stretch forth Your hand against the wrath
  of my enemies, and Your right hand will save me. The
  Lord will perfect that which concerns me; Your mercy
  and loving-kindness, O Lord, endure forever—forsake
  not the works of Your own hands. (Psalm 138:7–8)
- Now may our Lord Jesus Christ Himself and God our
  Father, Who loved us and gave us everlasting consolation and encouragement and well-founded hope through
  [His] grace (unmerited favor), comfort and encourage
  your hearts and strengthen them [make them steadfast
  and keep them unswerving] in every good work and
  word. (2 Thessalonians 2:16–17)

When you need peace

- You will guard him and keep him in perfect and constant peace whose mind [both its inclination and its

character] is stayed on You, because he commits himself to You, leans on You, and hopes confidently in You. (Isaiah 26:3)

- For though the mountains should depart and the hills be shaken or removed, yet My love and kindness shall not depart from you, nor shall My covenant of peace and completeness be removed, says the Lord, Who has compassion on you. (Isaiah 54:10)

- Peace I leave with you; My [own] peace I now give and bequeath to you. Not as the world gives do I give to you. Do not let your hearts be troubled, neither let them be afraid. [Stop allowing yourselves to be agitated and disturbed; and do not permit yourselves to be fearful and intimidated and cowardly and unsettled.] (John 14:27)

- And God's peace [shall be yours, that tranquil state of a soul assured of its salvation through Christ, and so fearing nothing from God and being content with its earthly lot of whatever sort that is, that peace] which transcends all understanding shall garrison and mount guard over your hearts and minds in Christ Jesus. (Philippians 4:7)

- Now may the Lord of peace Himself grant you His peace (the peace of His kingdom) at all times and in all ways [under all circumstances and conditions, whatever comes]. The Lord [be] with you all. (2 Thessalonians 3:16)

When you need forgiveness

- Have mercy upon me, O God, according to Your steadfast love; according to the multitude of Your tender mercy and loving-kindness blot out my transgressions. Wash me thoroughly [and repeatedly] from my iniquity and guilt and cleanse me and make me wholly pure from my sin! (Psalm 51:1–2)

- Purify me with hyssop, and I shall be clean [ceremonially]; wash me, and I shall [in reality] be whiter than snow. Make me to hear joy and gladness and be satisfied; let the bones which You have broken rejoice. Hide Your face from my sins and blot out all my guilt and iniquities. (Psalm 51:7–9)

- But He was wounded for our transgressions, He was bruised for our guilt and iniquities; the chastisement [needful to obtain] peace and well-being for us was upon Him, and with the stripes [that wounded] Him we are healed and made whole. (Isaiah 53:5)

When you feel guilty and condemned

- Therefore, [there is] now no condemnation (no adjudging guilty of wrong) for those who are in Christ Jesus, who live [and] walk not after the dictates of the flesh, but after the dictates of the Spirit. For the law of the Spirit of life [which is] in Christ Jesus [the law of our new being] has freed me from the law of sin and of death. (Romans 8:1–2)

- But if Christ lives in you, [then although] your [natural] body is dead by reason of sin and guilt, the spirit is alive because of [the] righteousness [that He imputes to you]. (Romans 8:10)

- Who shall bring any charge against God's elect [when it is] God Who justifies [that is, Who puts us in right relation to Himself? Who shall come forward and accuse or impeach those whom God has chosen? Will God, Who acquits us?] (Romans 8:33)

- For our sake He made Christ [virtually] to be sin Who knew no sin, so that in and through Him we might become [endued with, viewed as being in, and examples of] the righteousness of God [what we ought to be, approved and acceptable and in right relationship with Him, by His goodness]. (2 Corinthians 5:21)

When you need humility

- He leads the humble in what is right, and the humble He teaches His way. (Psalm 25:9)
- The Lord lifts up the humble and downtrodden; He casts the wicked down to the ground. (Psalm 147:6)
- Blessed (happy, to be envied, and spiritually prosperous—with life-joy and satisfaction in God's favor and salvation, regardless of their outward conditions) are the poor in spirit (the humble, who rate themselves insignificant), for theirs is the kingdom of heaven! (Matthew 5:3)

When you feel weak

- I have told you these things, so that in Me you may have [perfect] peace and confidence. In the world you have tribulation and trials and distress and frustration; but be of good cheer [take courage; be confident, certain, undaunted]! For I have overcome the world. [I have

deprived it of power to harm you and have conquered it
for you.] (John 16:33)

When you need justice

- Righteousness and justice are the foundation of Your
  throne; mercy and loving-kindness and truth go before
  Your face. (Psalm 89:14)
- Vengeance is Mine, and recompense, in the time when
  their foot shall slide; for the day of their disaster is at hand
  and their doom comes speedily (Deuteronomy 32:35)
- Therefore return to your God! Hold fast to love and
  mercy, to righteousness and justice, and wait [expec-
  tantly] for your God continually! (Hosea 12:6)
- Do not judge and criticize and condemn others, so that
  you may not be judged and criticized and condemned
  yourselves. For just as you judge and criticize and condemn others, you will be judged and criticized and condemned, and in accordance with the measure you [use
  to] deal out to others, it will be dealt out again to you.
  (Matthew 7:1–2)
- Vindicate me, O Lord, for I have walked in my integrity;
  I have [expectantly] trusted in, leaned on, and relied on the
  Lord without wavering and I shall not slide. (Psalm 26:1)
- For the Lord will judge and vindicate His people, and He
  will delay His judgments [manifesting His righteousness
  and mercy] and take into favor His servants [those who
  meet His terms of separation unto Him]. (Psalm 135:14)
- Do not let yourself be overcome by evil, but overcome
  (master) evil with good. (Romans 12:21)

When you need wisdom

- The reverent fear and worship of the Lord is the beginning of Wisdom and skill [the preceding and the first essential, the prerequisite and the alphabet]; a good understanding, wisdom, and meaning have all those who do [the will of the Lord]. Their praise of Him endures forever. (Psalm 111:10)

- Lean on, trust in, and be confident in the Lord with all your heart and mind and do not rely on your own insight or understanding. In all your ways know, recognize, and acknowledge Him, and He will direct and make straight and plain your paths. Be not wise in your own eyes; reverently fear and worship the Lord and turn [entirely] away from evil. (Proverbs 3 :5–7)

- Happy (blessed, fortunate, enviable) is the man who finds skillful and godly Wisdom, and the man who gets understanding [drawing it forth from God's Word and life's experiences], for the gaining of it is better than the gaining of silver, and the profit of it better than fine gold. Skillful and godly Wisdom is more precious than rubies; and nothing you can wish for is to be compared to her. (Proverbs 3:13–15)

- Hear counsel, receive instruction, and accept correction, that you may be wise in the time to come. (Proverbs 19:20)

- If any of you is deficient in wisdom, let him ask of the giving God [Who gives] to everyone liberally and ungrudgingly, without reproaching or faultfinding, and it will be given him. (James 1:5)

When you need self-control

- For God did not give us a spirit of timidity (of coward-ice, of craven and cringing and fawning fear), but [He has given us a spirit] of power and of love and of calm and well-balanced mind and discipline and self-control. (2 Timothy 1:7)

- Do not be quick in spirit to be angry or vexed, for anger and vexation lodge in the bosom of fools. (Ecclesiastes 7:9)

- Everything is permissible (allowable and lawful) for me; but not all things are helpful (good for me to do, expedient and profitable when considered with other things). Everything is lawful for me, but I will not become the slave of anything or be brought under its power. (1 Corinthians 6:12)

- Love endures long and is patient and kind; love never is envious nor boils over with jealousy, is not boastful or vainglorious, does not display itself haughtily. It is not conceited (arrogant and inflated with pride); it is not rude (unmannerly) and does not act unbecomingly. Love (God's love in us) does not insist on its own rights or its own way, for it is not self-seeking; it is not touchy or resentful; it takes no account of the evil done to it [it pays no attention to a suffered wrong]. (1 Corinthians 13:4–5)

- But the fruit of the [Holy] Spirit [the work which His presence within accomplishes] is love, joy (gladness), peace, patience (an even temper, forbearance), kindness, goodness (benevolence), faithfulness, gentleness (meekness, humility), self-control (self-restraint, continence). Against such things there is no law [that can bring a charge]. (Galatians 5:22–23)

When you have suffered loss

- Blessed be the God and Father of our Lord Jesus Christ, the Father of sympathy (pity and mercy) and the God [Who is the Source] of every comfort (consolation and encouragement), Who comforts (consoles and encourages) us in every trouble (calamity and affliction) so that we may also be able to comfort (console and encourage) those who are in any kind of trouble or distress, with the comfort (consolation and encouragement) with which we ourselves are comforted (consoled and encouraged) by God. (2 Corinthians 1:3–4)

- Blessed are those who mourn, for they will be comforted. (Matthew 5:4 NIV)

- Yes, though I walk through the [deep, sunless] valley of the shadow of death, I will fear or dread no evil, for You are with me; Your rod [to protect] and Your staff [to guide], they comfort me. (Psalm 23:4)

- They who sow in tears shall reap in joy and singing. (Psalm 126:5)

- And their life shall be like a watered garden, and they shall not sorrow or languish any more at all. Then will the maidens rejoice in the dance, and the young men and old together. For I will turn their mourning into joy and will comfort them and make them rejoice after their sorrow. (Jeremiah 31:11–13)

- For I know the thoughts and plans that I have for you,

says the Lord, thoughts and plans for welfare and peace
and not for evil, to give you hope in Your final outcome.
(Jeremiah 29:11)

When you're facing a new challenge

- The Lord is my Light and my Salvation—whom shall I
  fear or dread? The Lord is the Refuge and Stronghold of
  my life—of whom shall I be afraid? (Psalm 27:1)

- Be strong, courageous, and firm; fear not nor be in terror
  before them, for it is the Lord your God Who goes with
  you; He will not fail you or forsake you. (Deuteronomy
  31:6)

- Wait and hope for and expect the Lord; be brave and of
  good courage and let your heart be stout and enduring.
  Yes, wait for and hope for and expect the Lord. (Psalm
  27:14)

- I have strength for all things in Christ Who empowers me [I am ready for anything and equal to anything
  through Him Who infuses inner strength into me;
  I am self-sufficient in Christ's sufficiency]. (Philippians
  4:13)

- For we have become fellows with Christ (the Messiah)
  and share in all He has for us, if only we hold our first
  newborn confidence and original assured expectation
  [in virtue of which we are believers] firm and unshaken
  to the end. (Hebrews 3:14)

- [Urged on] by faith, Abraham, when he was called,
  obeyed and went forth into a place which he was des-
  tined to receive as an inheritance; and he went, although

he did not know or trouble his mind about where he was to go. (Hebrews 11:8)

When you are facing temptation

- God is our Refuge and Strength [mighty and impenetrable to temptation], a very present and well-proved help in trouble. (Psalm 46:1)

- In the day when I called, You answered me; and You strengthened me with strength (might and inflexibility to temptation) in my inner self. (Psalm 138:3)

- Teach me to do Your will, for You are my God; let your good Spirit lead me into a level country and into the land of uprightness. (Psalm 143:10)

- My son, if sinners entice you, do not consent. (Proverbs 1:10)

- My son, do not walk in the way with them; restrain your foot from their path, for their feet run to evil, and they make haste to shed blood. (Proverbs 1:16)

- Enter not into the path of the wicked, and go not in the way of evil men. Avoid it, do not go on it; turn from it and pass on. (Proverbs 4:14–15)

- Keep awake and watch and pray [constantly], that you may not enter into temptation; the spirit indeed is willing, but the flesh is weak. (Mark 14:38)

- And when He came to the place, He said to them, Pray that you may not [at all] enter into temptation. (Luke 22:40)

- Do not let yourself be overcome by evil, but overcome (master) evil with good. (Romans 12:21)

- Blessed (happy, to be envied) is the man who is patient under trial and stands up under temptation, for when he has stood the test and been approved, he will receive [the victor's] crown of life which God has promised to those who love Him. (James 1:12)
- So be subject to God. Resist the devil [stand firm against him], and he will flee from you. (James 4:7)

When you need to improve your thinking

- Lean on, trust in, and be confident in the Lord with all your heart and mind and do not rely on your own insight or understanding. In all your ways know, recognize, and acknowledge Him, and He will direct and make straight and plain your paths. (Proverbs 3:5–6)
- Do not be conformed to this world (this age), [fashioned after and adapted to its external, superficial customs], but be transformed (changed) by the [entire] renewal of your mind [by its new ideals and its new attitude], so that you may prove [for yourselves] what is the good and acceptable and perfect will of God, even the thing which is good and acceptable and perfect [in His sight for you]. (Romans 12:2)
- Strip yourselves of your former nature [put off and discard your old unrenewed self] which characterized your previous manner of life and becomes corrupt through lusts and desires that spring from delusion; and be constantly renewed in the spirit of your mind [having a fresh mental and spiritual attitude], and put on the new nature (the regenerate self) created in God's image,

[Godlike] in true righteousness and holiness. (Ephesians 4:22–24)

- For the rest, brethren, whatever is true, whatever is worthy of reverence and is honorable and seemly, whatever is just, whatever is pure, whatever is lovely and lovable, whatever is kind and winsome and gracious, if there is any virtue and excellence, if there is anything worthy of praise, think on and weigh and take account of these things [fix your minds on them]. (Philippians 4:8)

ABOUT THE AUTHOR

JOYCE MEYER is one of the world's leading practical Bible teachers. A #1 *New York Times* bestselling author, she has written more than ninety inspirational books, including *Do Yourself a Favor...Forgive, Living Beyond Your Feelings,* the entire Battlefield of the Mind family of books, and two novels, *The Penny* and *Any Minute,* as well as many others. She has also released thousands of audio teachings, as well as a complete video library. Joyce's *Enjoying Everyday Life®* radio and television programs are broadcast around the world, and she travels extensively conducting conferences. Joyce and her husband, Dave, are the parents of four grown children and make their home in St. Louis, Missouri.

JOYCE MEYER MINISTRIES
U.S. & FOREIGN OFFICE ADDRESSES

Joyce Meyer Ministries
P.O. Box 655
Fenton, MO 63026
USA
(636) 349-0303
www.joycemeyer.org

Joyce Meyer Ministries—Canada
P.O. Box 7700
Vancouver, BC V6B 4E2
Canada
(800) 868-1002

Joyce Meyer Ministries—Australia
Locked Bag 77
Mansfield Delivery Centre
Queensland 4122
Australia
(07) 3349 1200

Joyce Meyer Ministries—England
P.O. Box 1549
Windsor SL4 1GT
United Kingdom
01753 831102

Joyce Meyer Ministries—South Africa
P.O. Box 5
Cape Town 8000
South Africa
(27) 21-701-1056

OTHER BOOKS BY JOYCE MEYER

JOYCE MEYER SPANISH TITLES

Cambia Tus Palabras, Cambia Tu Vida

Come la Galleta... Compra los Zapatos (Eat the Cookie...
Buy the Shoes)

El Campo de Batalla de la Mente (Battlefield of the Mind)

La Revolución de Amor (The Love Revolution)

Las Siete Cosas Que Te Roban el Gazo (Seven Things
That Steal Your Joy)

Pensamientos de Poder (Power Thoughts)

BOOKS BY DAVE MEYER

Life Lines

* Study Guide available for this title